The CROSS and the OLIVE TREE

The CROSS and the OLIVE TREE

Cultivating Palestinian Theology amid Gaza

JOHN S. MUNAYER
SAMUEL S. MUNAYER

EDITORS

ORBIS BOOKS
Maryknoll, New York

Second Printing, October 2025

Founded in 1970, Orbis Books endeavors to publish works that enlighten the mind, nourish the spirit, and challenge the conscience. The publishing arm of the Maryknoll Fathers and Brothers, Orbis seeks to explore the global dimensions of the Christian faith and mission, to invite dialogue with diverse cultures and religious traditions, and to serve the cause of reconciliation and peace. The books published reflect the views of their authors and do not represent the official position of the Maryknoll Society. To learn more about Maryknoll and Orbis Books, please visit our website at www.orbisbooks.com.

Manufactured in the United States of America

Library of Congress Cataloging-in-Publication Data

Names: Munayer, John S. editor | Munayer, Samuel S. editor
Title: The cross and the olive tree : cultivating Palestinian theology
    amid Gaza / John S. Munayer, Samuel S. Munayer, editors.
Description: Maryknoll, NY : Orbis Books, [2025] | Includes
    bibliographical references and index. | Summary: "A collection of
    essays of Palestinian Christian theology" — Provided by publisher.
Identifiers: LCCN 2025016048 (print) | LCCN 2025016049 (ebook) |
    ISBN 9781626986343 paperback | ISBN 9798888660898 epub
Subjects: LCSH: Theology — Palestine
Classification: LCC BT30.P19 C76 2025 (print) | LCC BT30.P19
    (ebook) | DDC 230.095694 — dc23/eng/20250602
LC record available at https://lccn.loc.gov/2025016048
LC ebook record available at https://lccn.loc.gov/2025016049

*To the Palestinian People –
to the elders who have carried the cross
through endless Nakbas, and to the mothers and
fathers who cradle their children amid the ruins.
Like the olive tree rooted deep in our land,
your steadfast presence tells the story
of generations.*

*To those pressed from their lands like oil
from the olive, carrying its essence
across time and place.*

*To those who endured unbearable loss
yet remain standing, like olive trees
weathering drought.*

*To the children whose laughter was stolen –
you are the tender shoots sprouting
from roots centuries deep.*

*To the loved ones we have lost,
your memories will remain for us forever.*

*And to those who remain –
carrying forward both the cross of witness
and the wisdom of our ancestors,
continuing to be salt and light
in our land.*

Contents

Foreword

NAIM ATEEK AND CEDAR DUAYBIS

The genesis of this book goes back to the contemporary lived experience of all the young contributors to this volume. Undoubtedly, their parents, grandparents, or relatives must have experienced the 1948 Nakba when the State of Israel was founded. It was when we Palestinians, the Indigenous people of the land, were devastated as we lived through the destruction of our country and when our hopes and dreams for independence and sovereignty were dashed.

Indeed, the roots of the Palestinian-Israeli conflict go back to Theodore Hertzl in 1897 and the emergence of the Zionist Movement. He dreamed and worked hard for the establishment of a Jewish state in Palestine but failed to see its establishment during his lifetime.

For the Zionists, such a dream came to fruition in 1948 with the help and support of the major Western victorious powers of World War II, namely, the British Empire and the United States. The ensuing political conspiracies, intrigues, deceptions, and manipulations that were utilized by those powers in order to push forward the creation of the State of Israel have been covered by many conscientious Jewish, Palestinian, and Western scholars. By the end of the Palestinian-Israeli war in 1949, when the Armistice lines were drawn, some 80 percent of the Palestinians were evicted from their homes and lands, and were dispossessed of their properties. They were condemned to a life as refugees in the neighboring Arab countries as well as scattered throughout the world.

To put this into contextual perspective, both writers of this Foreword were part of the generation that, as children, lived through the experience of the first Nakba. In fact, the political catastrophe was a seismic shake-up for many of our long-held Christian beliefs. It was only after about forty years that we were able to articulate a theology of liberation that made sense of, and addressed, the theological, spiritual, political, and social impact that confronted and almost shattered our beliefs in God.

In spite of our skepticism, questions, and confusion, we were able, by the grace of God, to articulate a Palestinian theology of liberation toward the end of the 1980s. This theology helped many of us to renew, deepen, and revitalize our faith rather than abandon it. It deepened our love and faith in God, but it also energized our commitment to work for truth and justice. Furthermore, by using the hermeneutic of Christ, we were able to critique the powers of injustice, falsehood, deceit, and domination, and begin to advocate for a just peace based on biblical truths, United Nations resolutions, and international law. Moreover, Palestinian liberation theology helped us to address our own fears and prejudices, as well as confront and challenge the evils of ethnic supremacy, racism, and bigotry as we lived first under military law and then under the illegal Israeli occupation.

As mentioned above, this book is the fruit of the experience of a new generation of young Palestinian Christian scholars and theologians who have been experiencing a new Nakba at the hands of the present extreme, right-wing Israeli government that has far exceeded in its ferocity and carnage the 1948 catastrophe. It has become obviously clear that the hatred and animosity expressing itself through the Israeli army's genocidal warfare in the Gaza Strip has resulted so far in over fifty thousand dead and one hundred thousand injured, the majority of whom are women and children. This is not to mention the over seventeen thousand orphaned children and countless maimed for life. Over 90 percent of the structures in the Gaza Strip have been demolished totally or partially, including homes, schools and universities, hospitals, libraries, cultural centers and museums, plus several mosques and churches.

In addition to the situation in Gaza, Palestinians in the West Bank and East Jerusalem are being subjected to the most brutal measures by the Israeli army, supported by the religious extremist settlers.

Palestinian liberation theology emphasizes that authentic theological reflection cannot be disconnected from the political and social realities on the ground. Whereas in the upheaval of 1948 our held beliefs clashed with the reality of our lives under occupation, reading the Bible through Palestinian eyes and focusing on Jesus's life and teachings in Palestine under Roman occupation led us to Jesus's way of nonviolent resistance. This also liberated us and our theology from any elements of exclusion and racism and rooted us in the love of God and neighbor.

This book looks at the theological reflections of eight up-and-coming young theologians who are grappling with one of the most excruciating times in the history of our country. As mentioned already, the authors of these chapters found themselves facing an even more brutal and devastating Nakba than that of 1948. In fact, it has been an ongoing Nakba that culminated in the devastating events of October 7, 2023, and the following genocidal, fifteen-month war on Gaza.

These authors talk of the history of Christianity in the tiny Gaza Strip and of the lived faith of the people. They compare, analyze, and learn from other contexts that have endured similar conditions of colonialism and oppression. But most of all, they seek to keep people's hope alive by practicing a prophetic imagination of a brighter future based on our calling to build God's Kingdom on earth. Nowhere is such a vision more needed now than in Palestine-Israel, where Judaism and Christianity originated and where the political and social realities on the ground keep shifting like quicksand, for "without a vision, the people perish" (Proverbs 29:18, KJV).

One of the authors speaks about "co-resistance" as a way of bringing people across religious and ethnic boundaries to work and witness together in the face of oppression and injustice. Others rightly point out that whereas the number of Christians in the Holy Land is constantly declining (which is a matter of great concern), we have a moral and spiritual vocation to keep a living Christian presence in the land.

Another challenge that we must be aware of is the continuous need for Palestinian biblical scholars and theologians who can work on biblical interpretation and exegesis through the lens of liberation theology. This is of the utmost importance. Some of us have already done some writing in this area, but much more is needed. Many Christians as well as non-Christians are ignorant about the understanding and interpretation of the biblical texts that affect everyday life, whether for those who are living in the land or outside of it. As an example, one can cite the common saying that Israel is entitled to exclusive ownership of the land. This was one of the main challenges that faced the first generation of Palestinian liberation theologians. Although we dealt with it, further work needs to be done. We still need more biblically trained scholars who can present the true message of the Bible as rightly interpreted from both the Hebrew Scriptures and the New Testament, employing the Christ hermeneutic.

Reading these papers, one senses a Sumud (steadfastness), a different kind of Sumud, a "Sumud in faith" of these young thinkers in the face of a religious Zionist ideology that has blinded its adherents to any human rights pertaining to the Palestinians, let alone any respect for international law. Indeed, we find in these authors an inextinguishable hope that inspires the reader to believe that justice, peace, and reconciliation are achievable and that Christ's victory over the powers of evil and injustice can illuminate our path as we continue to strive for a future where all the people of our land can live in dignity, equality, and harmony.

Life is stronger than death. Resurrection and a new life of love and compassion are more enduring than injustice, bigotry, and domination.

Acknowledgments

This book is more than just the work of its editors and contributors; it is a collective effort made possible by the support, encouragement, and critical engagement of many individuals.

First and foremost, we extend our deepest gratitude to our parents, Salim and Kay. You are our foundation, and your love for us is extended in all that we do. Your wisdom, guidance, and steadfast support have shaped not only this book but our entire lives.

While we write this as a pair of brothers, we want to acknowledge another pair—Jack and Daniel. As older brothers, you have been role models, mentors, and a constant source of strength. This project, in many ways, is a shared endeavor between the four of us—a reflection of our bond and collective journey.

We are also deeply grateful to Rev. Dr. Naim Ateek, Ms. Cedar Duaybis, and Father David Neuhaus for their invaluable support, wisdom, and encouragement.

Finally, we extend our heartfelt thanks to the contributors for their dedication, time, and effort in shaping this work. We pray that, as Palestinian theologians, we remain united in faith and community, uplifting one another as we navigate the challenging road ahead.

Introduction

Palestinian Theology

JOHN S. MUNAYER AND SAMUEL S. MUNAYER

It is a great honor to introduce this book. At the same time, we wish we never had to write it. Writing about Palestinian theology amid genocide is neither an easy task nor does it give us any sense of pleasure. We wish this book did not have to exist, and the stakes of the book are undeniable. The weight is impossible to bear, and we feel that we cannot do justice to all the people who have been viciously killed. Fortunately, this burden is not carried alone. This is a joint effort of eight Palestinian theologians who come from all over Palestine: Gaza, Beit Sahour, Hebron, Nazareth, al-Lydd, and Jerusalem. We are all trying to wrestle with the tragedy unfolding around us and attempting to formulate it in theological language—yearning to utter Job's words, "I had heard of you by the hearing of the ear, but now my eye sees you" (Job 42:5). The contributors to this book have written their chapters as they watch their families being bombed and starved in Gaza, facing death threats, under erasure by a military occupation and a system of apartheid, and possibly facing punitive measures by the Israeli authorities for speaking out for justice and reconciliation.

Every word in this book is accompanied by the screams of children, images of destruction, bodies torn by violence, torture, and rape, stirring in us a profound sense of guilt rooted in our despair and the inability to stop the forces of evil. Alongside these horrors, the hypocrisy of the West, the incompetence of world leaders and international institutions, the gaslighting, the apathy of bystanders, and the performative activism done for self-importance or career advancement stir a deep sense of rage and disgust. Truly, the crucified people of Palestine are living the profound mystery of the cross under the weight of the empire. Mary's cries echo through the bereaved families.

We, Palestinian Christians, often call ourselves the living stones of the land of resurrection, believing in the good news of Christ. Yet leaping from Good Friday to Easter Sunday without fully entering the long silence of Holy Saturday may risk overlooking or even glorifying suffering. It feels as if God is absent in these moments, and we experience the paralyzing effects of fear with horrors still unfolding. Still, our faith calls us to love our enemy and remain faithful to the God of the oppressed, even when everything feels uncertain and dark. We hope, like Mary Magdalene, in the darkness and pain, that we, too, will one day discern the voice of resurrection, giving us the strength to endure and to empower others. Palestinian theology, like the narrative of the Bible, is encountered in these experiences. In essence, this book is written during crucifixion and in the expectant hope of resurrection.

Olive Trees and Palestinian Theology

As we write this introduction, it is the olive-picking season in Palestine. Olive trees are not just plants. They are spiritual entities, bearing both the pain and the beauty of our land with grace. Geries Khoury introduces Palestinian theology using the figure of olive trees: "Let me give you an image to illustrate local Palestinian theology. It is like the olive tree—

rooted in drought and stone, yet it endures. It lives for generations, growing steadfastly. Even when its branches are cut, new life emerges."[1] Therefore, in the spirit of this important season, we would like to extend Khoury's analogy of the olive tree by employing olive oil as an analogy through which to introduce Palestinian theology and to situate this book in the rich tradition of this heritage.

Every year since we can remember, we would pick olives as a family. We would then use our grandmother Samira's recipe to make enough olives to eat for the whole year, with plenty left over to share with friends. On one occasion, our grandfather Jacob visited us in our family's fields, which had been confiscated by the State of Israel. While too old to pick the olives, he told us about the painful experience of losing many olive tree groves in 1948, during the Nakba (Arabic for catastrophe). Our father made sure we listened as our grandfather continued in his storytelling, explaining how the family managed to find refuge in the Church of Saint George in the city of al-Lydd. In many ways, this simple tradition of picking olives went beyond simply making our annual supply of tasty olives. It connected us to the land, to our family history and roots, and to St. George, who for us represents indigenous Christianity in Palestine. Our family, the land, and theology are all intertwined, with one always informing the other.

The way that picking olives connects us to God, to our family, and to our roots serves as a metaphor for how Palestinian theology ought to connect us to God, to one another, our tradition, and our land. We understand theology as contemplation on and praxis in relation to the mystery of God. We also contend, as other liberation theology practitioners do,

---

1. Geries Khoury, "Theology of the Olive Tree Rooted in the Palestinian Land," in *Introduction to Palestinian Theology*, ed. Munther Isaac (Bethlehem: Diyar Press, 2018), 69–82. Translation by the authors.

that praxis and contemplation feed into one another.[2] In that sense, all people who talk about and act in relation to God are theologians. Like picking olives, all can be and are involved in such endeavors. We wish to break out of the assumption that theology is exclusive to those with formal education in churches and universities. Picking olives requires entire families and communities to be involved, and doing theology should not be any different. Khoury, when writing to Palestinians, comments that "Our (Palestinian) theology must be a communal theology."[3] In fact, theologians never operate as isolated individuals but are always part of a broader community and movement. Palestinian theologians should model Palestinian Falahin (Arabic for farmers or peasants), who work in community and for the community. Thus, the olive groves can be understood as the context in which the farmer/theologian does Palestinian theology.

Those who live in or have visited Palestine know how the geographical location affects the soil, water, minerals, and wind, which all play a vital role in the quality and character of the olives. Similarly, Palestinian theology will differ according to the contexts in which it is articulated and lived. While theologies in Palestine share a resemblance, they may take on different shapes, colors, and flavors according to the theological groves they are in.

The main component to be extracted from olives is oil, which can be used for several purposes, including religious rituals, medicine, soap, cooking, and lighting. Before we expand the fitting analogy of olive oil for the different

---

2. See, for example, Gustavo Gutiérrez, *On Job: God-Talk and the Suffering of the Innocent*, trans. Matthew J. O'Connell (New York: Orbis Books, 1987); Leonardo Boff, *Theology and Praxis: Epistemological Foundations*, trans. Robert R. Barr (Eugene, OR: Wipf & Stock, 1987); James H. Cone, *God of the Oppressed* (New York: Orbis Books, 1975).

3. Khoury, "Theology of the Olive Tree," 70.

categories of Palestinian theology, it is helpful to briefly discuss what qualifies as Palestinian oil/theology.

Not all olives in Palestine produce Palestinian olive oil. People might pick olives on stolen land, as the Israeli settlers do; some might export the olives outside of Palestine; and others may let the olives rot and fall off the trees. That is to say, not all theologians in Palestine are speaking/doing/living Palestinian theology. Palestinian theology is a theology that is made by Palestinians and for the sake of all people in Palestine: Jews, Christians, Muslims, and others. The lived Palestinian experience, encompassing both the oppression and suffering endured by Palestinians and the beauty, richness, imperfections, and complexities of their existence, is central to Palestinian theology. Likewise, the main message of the gospel is the liberation of all people from all captivity—physical and spiritual—and the inauguration of the Kingdom of God (Luke 4:16–21, 43). Hence, any theology in Palestine that does not promote liberation is not Palestinian theology. To that end, discernment is crucial when walking through the theological olive groves of Palestine, for "every good tree bears good fruit, but a bad tree bears bad fruit. A good tree cannot bear bad fruit, and a bad tree cannot bear good fruit" (Matthew 7:17–18).

Internationals are another important aspect of the theological olive groves of Palestine. Often, there are internationals who come to Palestine to help with the olive harvest. These people both contribute greatly to the workload and serve as a protective presence from Israeli soldiers and settlers. In a similar manner, international theologians have been extremely helpful in supporting the development and articulation of Palestinian theology. They have helped with writing, organizing, publishing, and funding.

With that said, Palestinians have also had a hard time with some volunteers during the olive harvest. Sometimes, internationals do not understand Palestinian norms, have a white savior mentality, or provoke Israeli soldiers in an unhelpful manner, putting Palestinians themselves at risk. By the same token, we have seen international theologians who have similarly missed the mark in the theological scene in Palestine. Some have not worked in a culturally sensitive way and have increased tensions within Palestinian theological circles. Even worse, a number of international theologians have claimed to represent a Palestinian voice abroad or built entire careers on the back of Palestinian theology. There is also a colonial phenomenon, specifically among North Americans and Europeans who either live in Palestine for a while or think they are familiar with the Palestinian Christian community, and who begin to tell us how to do our theology. As much as we appreciate the support and collaboration, internationals, especially white privileged theologians, need to know their place and their role.

Palestinian olive groves, olives, and olive oil can be helpful in articulating a Palestinian theology that is organic to the land and its people. Three primary uses of olive oil introduce the three main theological spheres in Palestine.

Church

Olive oil holds a significant role in Palestinian churches, symbolizing the presence of the Holy Spirit, health, anointing, and blessings. For example, the tomb of St. George in al-Lydd always contains olive oil, which visitors use to make the sign of the cross on their foreheads.[4] The presence of olive oil in Palestinian churches can be seen as a reflection of Palestinian theology itself — a theology deeply intertwined with the lived experiences of the Palestinian church. Despite its

---

4. Clayton Goodgame, "A Lineage in Land: The Transmission of Palestinian Christianity," *The Journal of the Royal Anthropological Institute* 29, no. 3 (2023): 670–91.

complexities, achievements, limitations, diversity, and struggles, the church in Palestine has, in some cases, remained a steadfast ecclesial body, carrying forth the witness of the faith since Pentecost.

For many Palestinian Christians, the clergy embody a theology that resonates with their daily lives, forming a central pillar in their understanding of the mystery of faith within the Palestinian context. The clergy, rooted in their communities and sharing a profound connection with their people, serve as "salt and light" in a land marked by adversities. Unlike the majority of clergy serving in the land, who are not from Palestine and often cannot speak the language, Palestinian clergy arise from within their communities, sharing both language and lived experience with their congregations. Through their prayers, sermons, statements, baptisms, weddings, and daily lives, some Palestinian clergy embody a form of theology that is shaped by and responsive to the needs and realities of their people. Like olive oil in the churches, they bless their people.

Emeritus Latin Patriarch Michel Sabbah, often called the "Patriarch of the People" by Palestinians, exemplifies the role of olive oil in the church as a symbol of blessing.[5] This title alone, "Patriarch of the People," reflects Sabbah's profound connection with his community. Through his sermons, prayers, pastoral letters, service to civil society, and commitment to interfaith relations, Sabbah has created a wealth of theological resources that have guided the Palestinian church in its witness from the First Intifada to the present day. His impact on Palestinian theology and the broader Palestinian community is undeniable, which explains the deep respect and affection he receives from the laity. Sab-

---

5. Habash Lily and Mohammed Alatar, "The Patriarch of the People: Reflections with the Patriarch," YouTube, 2020, https://www.youtube.com/watch?v=AuSuuaCHQPQ&t=585s.

bah's role as a source of blessing extends to other notable Palestinian clergy, such as Bishop Faik Haddad, Bishop Jamal Khader, Bishop Munib Younan, Father Rafiq Khoury, Rev. Fadi Diab, Rev. Alex Awad, Rev. Munther Isaac, Bishop Atallah Hanna, Bishop Sani Ibrahim Azar, Rev. Naim Ateek, Rev. Mitri Raheb, and others. This list of clergy highlights a diverse mosaic of voices, each bringing unique theological insights that, like olive oil in the church, attempt to bless all who enter, especially the oppressed.

However, olive oil in the church can also be obstructed from reaching the people. Often compromised by institutions that maintain the status quo or even support oppressive colonial structures, many Palestinian clergy operate within churches that contribute to the colonization of Palestine.[6] This dynamic spans many churches and denominations. These churches, along with their leaders, sometimes compromise their mission by aligning with structures of power and privilege, neglecting their duty to stand with the poor and oppressed. This reality is painfully visible amid the genocide in Gaza and throughout the 107 years of settler colonialism. The olive oil meant to bless is frequently diluted or, at times, entirely absent.

The churches in Palestine have become spaces of tension, where clergy (even Palestinian) may become both the good shepherd and the false teacher, standing as both anticolonial advocates and colonizer enablers, embodying both the olive oil of blessing and the vinegar offered to Christ on the cross. Yet, the spirit of blessing endures in the Palestinian church, and a nuanced approach is needed. To overlook the role, influence, and service of the church in Palestine is to

---

6. See Salim Tamari, *The Great War and the Remaking of Palestine* (Oakland: University of California Press, 2017); and Laura Robson, *Colonialism and Christianity in Mandate Palestine* (Austin: University of Texas Press, 2011).

miss the holistic understanding of Palestinian theology and its role in our times.

Soap

Academic Palestinian theology can be likened to the olive oil used to produce Nabulsi soap. Nablus, a city in Palestine, is renowned for this olive-oil soap, found in many Palestinian homes and exported globally. Nabulsi soap is highly valued for its organic composition, and its ability to cleanse the body of dirt and toxins. Similarly, academic theology serves as both an intellectual and spiritual cleanser, offering a liberating interpretation of the Christian faith in response to the realities of settler colonization, occupation, and, more recently, genocide. This theology challenges narratives that misuse faith or Scripture to justify the oppression of Palestinians while addressing key issues such as justice, forgiveness, and reconciliation. One of the significant concerns Palestinian theologies engage with is the declining Christian population in a context where Islam and Judaism are the dominant religions.[7] This has made interfaith relations a central theme of Palestinian theological reflection and practice. Palestinian theology is also informed by the broader Mashreq and North African contexts, acknowledging that, while these regions share similar historical and political challenges, each also faces unique circumstances.

At its core, Palestinian theology revolves around themes such as hermeneutics, justice, land, covenant, biblical prophecy, identity, resistance, and solidarity—themes that have deeply shaped the Palestinian experience.[8] Just as soap

---

7. See Rafiq Khoury, *Local Palestinian Theology (1965–2019): A Comprehensive Vision* (Bethlehem: Al-liqa Publications, 2019), translation by the authors.

8. See Munther Isaac, *Introduction to Palestinian Theology* (Bethlehem: Diyar Press, 2018), translation from Arabic by the authors; Rafiq Khoury, "Palestinian Contextual Theology: A General Survey,"

restores physical well-being, this form of Palestinian theology strives to restore spiritual and societal wholeness by confronting the sin of colonization and offering hermeneutical tools to uncover the pathway toward redemption witnessed in the Bible. Ultimately, this theology can be viewed as an intellectual effort to love God with our minds, by resisting oppression through the intellect and seeking the restoration of both people and land through a political and spiritual vision.

Academic Palestinian theology is not an exercise in abstractions or metaphysical speculation. Actual events shaped the roots and soil of Palestinian theology, including the Nakba of 1948. The Nakba profoundly impacted the collective Palestinian experience and identity, planting the seeds for the emergence of this theology.[9] The Naksa (Arabic for setback) in 1967 brought a new sense of urgency for Palestinian theology due to the rise of religious Zionist rhetoric, both Christian and Jewish, seeking to justify Palestinian colonization and intensifying the need for theological reflection on the realities of occupation and displacement.[10] The year 1967 represents a turning point for Palestinian theology, when it began articulating itself systematically. In addition, the indigenization of clergy in the 1970s, many of whom were and are professional theologians, further solidified the development of Palestinian theology. These pastor-scholars were able to address many of the theological questions with sustained reflection.[11]

The First Intifada (1987–1993) propelled Palestinian theology into the global spotlight, highlighting its liberative mes-

---

in *Christian Theology in the Palestinian Context*, ed. Rafiq Khoury and Rainer Zimmer-Winkel (Berlin: Aphorism A, 2019), 9–46.

9. Naim S. Ateek, *A Palestinian Theology of Liberation: The Bible, Justice, and the Palestinian-Israeli Conflict* (Maryknoll, NY: Orbis Books, 2017).

10. Ateek, *A Palestinian Theology of Liberation.*

11. Khoury, "Palestinian Contextual Theology," 17.

sage and its deep connection to the struggle for justice and peace.[12] This grassroots uprising, with the active involvement of Palestinian Christians, brought Palestinian theology to international attention, cementing its place in global discourse. During this time, theologians such as Rafiq Khoury, Geries Khoury, Naim Ateek, Mitri Raheb, Cedar Duaybis, Jean Zaru, Salim J. Munayer, Alex Awad, Nora Carmi, and others began to publish books, write articles, establish organizations, and convene conferences, expanding the reach of Palestinian theological thought.[13] The Second Intifada (2000–2005) further underscored the continued relevance of Palestinian theology, both for Palestinians and international audiences. Though these theologians addressed various topics, hailed from different regions, and targeted diverse audiences, they could be seen as the first wave of Palestinian Christian "soap makers," pioneers whose witness, wisdom, and influence continue to cleanse the Palestinian collective from the stain of colonial supremacy. This theology is not confined to ivory towers of academia. It is rooted in active engagement with the Palestinian community, demonstrating pragmatic versatility that transcends mere scholarly reflection.

Many of the students and mentees of the first wave of thinkers continued this form of Palestinian theology while developing it and exploring other topics: Munther Isaac, Niveen Sarras, Viola Raheb, Yohana Katanacho, and Grace Zougbi. Again, these theologians may not address the same questions or use the same methodologies, and, at times, they hold diverse perspectives; nevertheless, their development,

---

12. Ateek, *A Palestinian Theology of Liberation*, 34.

13. See, for example, *Faith and the Intifada: Palestinian Christian Voices*, ed. Naim S. Ateek, Rosemary Radford Ruether, and Marc Ellis (New York: Orbis Books, 1992); Elizabeth Marteijn, "The Revival of Palestinian Christianity: Developments in Palestinian Theology," *Exchange* 49, nos. 3–4 (2020): 257–77.

training, and institutional affiliations are connected to the early articulations of Palestinian theology.

As we reflect on the historical trajectory of Palestinian theology, recent events—the Unity Intifada in 2021,[14] the martyrdom of Shireen Abu-Akleh, the October 7 attack, the ongoing genocide in Gaza, and intensifying settler-colonial violence—have and will profoundly shape this tradition. These events are bringing new voices to the forefront of Palestinian theology, many of whom are contributors to this book. Like the founders, these emerging theologians are grappling with similar questions, striving to build on the witness and mission of Palestinian theology. These voices include Yousef AlKhouri, Shadia Qubti, Tony Deik, Lamma Mansour, Yasmine Rishmawi, Marah Sarji, Daniel Munayer, Daniel Bannoura, Azmera Hammouri-Davis, Anthony Khair, the editors of this book, and others. Importantly, some of these newer voices, whether explicitly or implicitly, are critically examining the tradition of Palestinian theology itself and attempting to build further on its foundations. They are seeking to illuminate limitations within and offer alternative ways for the tradition to better contribute to a roadmap of liberation, equality, reconciliation, and justice for all people living in the land. In other terms, they are making new olive-oil soap from inherited recipes.

Lamp

One of the most overlooked forms of Palestinian theology, both by Palestinians and internationals, is grassroots theology, or theology of the people, often expressed through lived

---

14. The Unity Intifada of 2021 refers to a collective Palestinian uprising that emerged in May 2021, characterized by widespread demonstrations, strikes, and nonviolent confrontations across multiple fronts in historical Palestine. See Lana Tatour, "The 'Unity Intifada' and 48 Palestinians: Between the Liberal and the Decolonial," *Journal of Palestinian Studies* 50, no. 4 (2020): 84–99.

religion. This theology can be likened to one of the most fundamental uses of olive oil throughout history: burning lamps to provide light. This type of oil is unfit for consumption and, therefore, is inexpensive and commonly used as fuel in households. Because it is accessible to most, it is valued for illuminating homes. In this way, the olive oil of lamps represents the theology of the people in Palestine, a theology formed in households and shaped by all family members.

This theology is neither less valuable than nor redundant with other forms of theology. Rather, Palestinian olive oil for theological lamps emphasizes abundance and the ability to shed light. This theology sheds light for most Palestinian Christians in times of profound darkness. The lived religion is witnessed through the veneration of saints, traditional rituals, holidays such as Easter (especially Sabt al-Nour), everyday greetings and expressions steeped in theological language, special foods prepared for occasions, poetry, iconography, and many other cultural practices in Palestine.[15] This theology is not confined to Christians but is also seen in our Muslim brothers and sisters. The olive tree and olive oil hold significant importance in Islam, as highlighted in Surah an-Nūr (The Chapter of Light, 24:35), where God's light is described as a lamp burning olive oil. Also the Prophet Muhammad instructed, "Eat the oil (of olives) and use it on your hair and skin, for it comes from a blessed tree" (Sunan al-Tirmidhi). Together, the lived theologies of Palestinians create a profound sense of identity and belonging within Palestinian communities, connecting people to the transcendent as rooted in the land. This can be understood as part of Palestinian indigeneity.

In the context of genocide and settler colonization, this form of theology both affirms the reality of Palestinian suf-

---

15. John S. Munayer and Samuel S. Munayer, "Decolonising Palestinian Liberation Theology: New Methods, Sources and Voices," *Studies in World Christianity* 28, no. 3 (2022): 287–310.

fering and celebrates Palestinian beauty, resilience, and joy, making it a form of resistance. Moreover, these practices offer a glimpse into how Palestinians imagine hope, process grief, and find meaning both politically and spiritually. Theology of the lamplight affirms Palestinian humanity within a context that denies it, especially when Palestinians are referred to as "human animals."[16] While it may not always directly counter oppressive ideologies like Zionism, this theology centers the Palestinian experience, seeking to offer light amid the darkness. Unlike a lot of Palestinian academic theology, Palestinian theology of the people is not meant for advocacy but promotes internal empowerment and connectedness.

Regrettably, some within colonized theological circles dismiss these practices as superstitions rather than legitimate theological expressions. Some Palestinian theologians may also undervalue this form of theology, perhaps too focused on creating liberationist interpretations to counter Christian Zionism (like olive-oil soap), or preparing sermons for the next Sunday (olive oil in the church). Yet not everyone needs to be a soap maker or prepare the olive oil for church services; olive oil for lamps is accessible to all.

When building a Palestinian theology of healing and liberation, this form of theology might be the most significant, resonating deeply with the people as it affirms their humanity daily and offers visions of redemption. Olive oil can be applied in many ways, but it is nonetheless from the same tree. This theology of the people arises in our homes and kitchens, from our elders and children, through our stories, and from the changing seasons—rather than from conferences, lectures, or books. Theology of the lamp is, perhaps,

---

16. The words of former defense minister Yoav Gallant when referring to the Palestinians in Gaza, MEE Staff, "Israel-Palestine War: 'We Are Fighting Human Animals,' Israeli Defense Minister Says," *Middle East Eye*, October 9, 2023, https://www.middleeasteye.net/news/israel-palestine-war-fighting-human-animals-defence-minister.

the most freely expressed Palestinian theology, unconfined by academic borders or church restrictions. This theology has impacted us most profoundly as we have borne witness to the spiritual encounters that our grandparents transmitted to us in the olive groves of al-Lydd. There, we encountered the sacred, the trauma, and the witness to love, all felt in our bodies and minds. So, given the power of this usage of olive oil, who holds the authority to determine who is or is not a theologian?

While we have described and introduced Palestinian theology as three different types of olive oil, these categories are not mutually exclusive. They are merely here to help orient one in the field of Palestinian theology, highlighting the nuances so we can appreciate the multilayered beauty of the theological olive grove. These distinctions help us avoid oversimplifications, resist concentration on individuals, and appreciate the mosaic of diversity in Palestinian theology. Palestinian theology is more than a reactionary response to Christian Zionism. One can certainly be more active or influenced by a certain category of Palestinian theology, but one is not bound to it. Palestinians use each of the three olive oils, just in different ways and portions. What is certain is that the olive oil that is produced, whether for lamps or soap, bears the influence of olives harvested from trees now soaked in the blood and tears of many.

The Book: The Cross and the Olive Tree

This book and its collection of chapters have been influenced by all types of oil in Palestine: theology of the people, academics, and clergy. Likewise, it is deeply influenced by the current climate for the olive trees, namely, genocide. While the daily realities of destruction, ethnic cleansing, and loss have persisted for over 107 years, the current events in Gaza reflect an unprecedented scale of devastation. Genocide is more than a legal category in international law. It is a harrowing symbol of reality that has taken shape since 1917. Genocide has been forced into public consciousness since October 2023, carrying profound implications at both individual and global levels.[17]

Doing theology amid genocide speaks both to the immediate destruction in Gaza and to the irreversible transformation of perspectives worldwide, including within ourselves. It is why the cross, symbolizing the Christian faith, and the olive tree, symbolizing Palestine, interpret each other, each shedding light on the other's reality. All the authors are committed to continuing the legacy of our tradition, paved by our theological forebears. Indeed, the influence on this book also goes beyond Palestine, drawing from other theologies and theologians from different oppressed and colonized contexts. As unimaginable suffering is inflicted on our people and the land we so love, Palestinian theology must ask itself difficult and pressing questions. It must be relevant for the new and ever-changing realities in which we live. We must continue to make olive oil, in the good and bad seasons, as witnesses to the baptism, life, crucifixion, and resurrection of Jesus Christ. We must continue to make Palestinian olive oil so that we may be a blessing to our own people and our enemies as well.

As such, the book addresses key questions such as What is the theological and Christian legacy of Gaza? How is the theology of martyrdom relevant during these times? How can we exercise divine imagination? What might reconciliation look like during genocide? What can we learn from other communities that have gone through genocide, and how can we build transnational solidarity? Where is Christ during a genocide?

---

17. The book is written in English in order to engage with a wider audience but will be in Arabic for our own communities.

Teita's Faith

Yousef AlKhouri (Gaza/Bethlehem) highlights the history of Christianity in Gaza and the role of Jewish and Christian Zionism in the decline of its Christian population. Through his grandmother's experiences, he introduces "Teita theology," a grandmother theology, as a model of faith rooted in resilience and Jesus's teachings. This chapter, combining personal and interdisciplinary approaches, seeks to preserve the legacy of Palestinian Christians in Gaza, countering the destruction of knowledge in times of genocide.

Guatemala and Gaza

Marah Sarji (Nazareth) looks at some of the similarities and interconnectedness between the genocide in Palestine and Guatemala. She also examines both genocides from a gender and sexuality lens, highlighting the violence experienced by Palestinians, especially women, due to patriarchal violence. Sarji attempts to answer the question "Where are you, God?" — Wenak ya Allah? in Arabic — by locating Christ in the practices and ethics of care embodied by Guatemalan and Gazan women.

A New World Is Coming; She Is on Her Way

Azmera Hammouri-Davis (Hebron/Kea'au, Hawai'i) brings Palestinian and African American theology into conversation. She examines the ways in which both traditions can learn from each other, bringing both her unique expertise and identity into dialogue with the other. Furthermore, Hammouri-Davis examines the unique and powerful perspective of the womanist tradition and how it can support Palestinians who are experiencing a genocide. This chapter, similarly to those of Shadia Qubti and Sarji, makes a vital step to encourage dialogue between traditions that have faced and are still facing immense oppression due to white supremacy and colonial logics.

Imagination in the Valley of the Shadow of Death
Lamma Mansour (Nazareth) looks at how Palestinian Christians can use divine imagination as a form of faithful witness to the Kingdom of God during oppression and suffering. In the midst of such brutality and suffering, Mansour advocates for a divine imagination that allows us to live in relation to the future that God has planned. As such, she argues that divine imagination is not simply an abstract worldview, but praxis for survival, resistance, and collective action. Mansour focuses on three areas of divine imagination: (1) reclamation, (2) disruption, and (3) catalyst.

Reconciliation and Co-Resistance: A Redemptive Vision
Daniel S. Munayer (Jerusalem/al-Lydd) attempts to offer a theological and practical model of reconciliation in Palestine-Israel in times of genocide. Building on years of experience in the field of reconciliation, and theological engagement with biblical Scripture and theologians from other colonized contexts, Daniel argues for a decolonial understanding of reconciliation that works for liberation and the ultimate vision of redemption for all people. This chapter seeks to challenge both watered-down Western concepts of reconciliation and uncompromising Palestinian concepts of justice.

Noticing Sumac in Unexpected Places
Shadia Qubti (Nazareth) engages with the historical and theological developments among Palestinian and Indigenous Turtle Island theologians. Qubti focuses on the theological analysis of both sets of theologies on the concept of land. Qubti carefully compares and contrasts the two traditions and their engagement with colonial theology. The chapter does not simply suggest reading these two colonial contexts as mirrors of each other. Rather, it engages in both

similarities and differences, and provides insights for future dialogue. Qubti's deep knowledge of both traditions, each having endured its own genocide, provides a foundation for fostering greater transnational solidarity among colonized peoples.

Palestinian Theology of Martyrdom

We, Samuel S. Munayer and John S. Munayer (Jerusalem/ al-Lydd), attempt to articulate a Palestinian theology of martyrdom. Given the death of so many, including Gazan Christians who have been and continue to be faithful witnesses to the Kingdom of God, we seek to explore what faithful martyrdom looks like in Palestine. In this chapter, we will build on Scripture and the Christian tradition to challenge the "theology of survival," encourage communal witness, and redefine the "signs of our time."

In conclusion, we invite the reader to dive into each chapter and reflect with great patience and detail over what the authors are asking, arguing, and articulating. We invite the readers to walk with us in the olive groves of Palestinian theology. Pay attention to the smells, sights, tastes, and feelings of the olives we are picking. Witness as we attempt to make relevant olive oil for our current reality. As our people are being slaughtered, starved, expelled, and arrested, we seek to make sense of our experience. We do this not only for our own sake as theologians but for the sake of participating in God's liberative work in history. We bring our pain, which is becoming deeper and wider, into conversation with each other and God in this book. And our anger, which is at a boiling point beyond imagination, is our motivation to continue the work in Palestine in order to see liberation and reconciliation.

We expect to see our situation deteriorate and do not

know what the future holds. Nevertheless, we wish to be faithful witnesses to the gospel, just as the ultimate Samid (steadfast one), Jesus Christ, showed us.[18]

---

18. Munayer and Munayer, "Decolonising Palestinian Liberation Theology," 304.

1

Teita's Faith

The Story of Palestinian Christians in Gaza through the Eyes of Grandmothers

YOUSEF KAMAL ALKHOURI
Gaza and Bethlehem

The Gaza Strip, a small Palestinian coastal territory on the Mediterranean, is often associated with conflict in modern times, overshadowing its long and rich history. While much has been written about the region's geopolitical struggles, little attention has been given to Gaza's Christian heritage.[1] This chapter aims to partially fill that gap by exploring the Christian history of Gaza, its churches, and community, alongside the alarming decline of its Christian population in recent years. I argue that Zionist settler-colonial ideology — both Jewish and Christian — has played a pivotal role in this decline. Yet, despite the immense challenges they face, Gaza's Christians offer an inspiring example of faith and resilience. The stories of my grandmothers — teitas in Arabic — who offer a sincere commitment to the teachings of Jesus, are central to

---

1. See, for example, Aref Al-Aref, *Tārīkh Ghazza* (Jerusalem: Dar al-Aytam al-Islamiyya, 1943); Saleem Arafat Mubayad, *al-Nasraniyya wa atharha fi Ghazza wa ma hawlaha* (Ghazza: Yazji Bookshop Publishers, 1998); Abaher El Sakka, *Gaza: A Social History under British Colonial Rule, 1917–1948* (Beirut: Institute of Palestine Studies, 2018).

this chapter. Their love for both neighbors and enemies is a witness and testimony of a genuine faith.

This chapter introduces Teita Faith, a model of faithfulness grounded in the lived experiences of Palestinian grandmothers amid suffering.[2] By employing a cross-disciplinary approach rooted in postcolonial tradition, it examines Gaza's Christian history at the intersection of history, politics, and theology. To provide the necessary context, I first offer a survey of the Christian history of Gaza, followed by an exploration of the current realities facing Palestinian Christians, particularly the factors contributing to their rapid decline. I argue that Zionism, both Jewish and Christian, has been instrumental in the displacement and marginalization of Palestinian Christians in Gaza. In the final section, I introduce Teita Faith, framed through the personal stories of my grandmothers.

But Why Grandmothers?

Grandmothers play a vital role in the transmission of history, faith, and values. Refaat Alareer, a Palestinian poet and scholar who was tragically killed in an Israeli airstrike in 2023, underscores the ways his grandmother shaped his understanding of their family and national history in his 2015 TED Talk. He argues that grandmothers, as storytellers, "inject these stories with values and meanings," becoming agents between the past and the present.[3] Alareer's state-

---

2. Lamma Mansour (PhD, Oxford University), a friend and contributor to this volume, introduced me to the concept of *teita* theology and Kat Armas's work *Abuelita Faith* during one of our meetings in preparation for this publication. After I shared how my grandmothers shaped my faith and understanding of Palestinian Christian history, she encouraged me to explore the idea of writing a *teita* theology. I am deeply grateful for Dr. Mansour's wisdom and insight.

3. Refaat Alareer, "Stories Make Us," *TEDxShujaiy*, 16 November 2015, https://www.youtube.com/watch?v=YsbEjldJjOw.

ment highlights the importance of their stories as an integral part of the oral history of Palestine, and particularly of Nakba.[4] Those stories encompass a memory of individuals, the "collective, and the nation."[5] Memory and oral history are frequently intertwined. Oral history is also "a social history of people, communities, places, and events."[6] The rise of feminism in the second half of the twentieth century brought about the recognition of women's role in "making their socio-economic, political and cultural history."[7] Women, hence, play a focal role in the making of and contributing to religious and spiritual history.

The stories of teitas are historical and faith-based testimonies. I focus on my maternal grandmother, Jamila, using her experiences as a lens to understand Palestinian Christian displacement during the Nakba of 1948 and its aftermath. Additionally, I reflect on my paternal grandmother, Naima, who was a catalyst for peace and reconciliation. These narratives are vital due to the imminent loss of the first generation of the Nakba survivors and because, as Kat Armas highlights in *Abuelita Faith* (2021), women like my grandmothers—abuelitas in Spanish, teitas in Arabic—are "women who bear the scars of colonization."[8] Their theological reflections emerge

4. American University of Beirut, *Palestinian Oral History Archive*, https://libraries.aub.edu.lb/poha.

5. Lynn Abrams, *Oral History Theory*, 2nd ed. (London and New York: Routledge, 2016), 79.

6. Thomas M. Ricks, "Perspectives on the Endless Nakba: Palestinian Oral History and Traumatic Memory," *Jerusalem Quarterly* 90 (2022): 122, https://www.palestine-studies.org/sites/default/files/jq-articles/Perspectives%20on%20the%20Endless%20Nakba.pdf.

7. Nahla Abdo, "Feminism, Indigenousness and Settler Colonialism: Oral History, Memory and the Nakba," in *An Oral History of the Palestinian Nakba*, ed. Nur Masalha and Nahla Abdo (London: Zed Books, 2018), 40–64 (41).

8. Kat Armas, *Abuelita Faith: What Women on the Margins Teach Us about Wisdom, Persistence, and Strength* (Grand Rapids, MI: Brazos Press, 2021), Kindle edition.

from real-life experiences of suffering and resilience, providing insights that are neither abstract nor theoretical but deeply rooted in the "real, raw outworking of faith."[9] Teita Faith is not "a lofty" or academic endeavor; instead, it offers the church a model of faithful obedience to Jesus's teachings, particularly amidst torment.[10]

It is important to note that I write this essay as a Gazan Christian living in Bethlehem, with close family members still sheltering in Gaza's churches after months of violence (as of November 2024). I rely on both personal accounts from Palestinian Christians still residing in Gaza and a combination of primary and secondary sources to construct this historical narrative. I am mindful of the gendered lens of this work. As Kat Armas rightly observes, "Too often, women — particularly marginalized women — are the heroines of someone else's story, or worse yet, someone else (usually a man) is the hero of theirs."[11] I do not position myself as a hero in this narrative. I wish to emphasize that teitas are the true heroines of faith, preserving a legacy that we Palestinians cannot afford to lose.

The Story of Christianity in Gaza

On December 19, 2023, in response to a question by a journalist about the Israeli killing of two Palestinian Christian women who were sheltering in the Church of the Holy Family, the Israeli deputy mayor of Jerusalem confidently stated, "There are no churches in Gaza."[12] Her comment came either out of ignorance or mere denial. But, arguably, this sentiment is widespread also among Western Christians.

---

9. Armas, *Abuelita Faith*.
10. Armas, *Abuelita Faith*.
11. Armas, *Abuelita Faith*.
12. Emma Soteriou, "No Christians in Gaza, Claims Jerusalem Deputy Mayor after Israeli Army Kills Two Women at Church," *LBC*, 19 December 2023, https://www.lbc.co.uk/news/no-christians-church-gaza-jerusalem-deputy-mayor-israeli-army-kills-two.

Churches have been built in Gaza since the early centuries of Christianity, and a few remain until the present day. My teitas consistently shared stories about the deep roots of the Christian community and its rich heritage in Gaza.[13] With great pride, they spoke of thirty-six generations of priests who came from our family. To honor this legacy, our family name became AlKhouri, meaning "the priest's family." The stories told by my teitas serve as a testament to the enduring Christian presence in Gaza, tracing back to the first century.

Located on strategic trade routes, Gaza connected the ancient world and its civilizations. Some scholars suggest that the Holy Family might have taken this route during their escape to Egypt (see Matthew 2:13–23). According to Coptic Church tradition, Joseph, Mary, and the baby Jesus passed through Gaza, Khan Yunis, and Rafah on their way to Egypt, fleeing the brutality of Herod.[14] Furthermore, an early oral Christian tradition among Gazan Christians states that the Holy Family rested under a sycamore tree in Gaza city.[15] In the New Testament, Philip's encounter with the Ethiopian eunuch was near Gaza (Acts 8:26–40). Martin A. Meyer proposes that Philip introduced Christianity to Gaza as early as the first century. Interestingly, Meyer also asserts that "tradition suggests the first bishop of the city was Philemon, the same to whom Paul addressed an epistle."[16] Given Gaza's strong ties to the Nabatean kingdom, and considering the friendship between Paul and Philemon, it raises the question whether the apostle Paul might have visited Gaza

13. Elizabeth S. Marteijn, "The Revival of Palestinian Christianity: Developments in Palestinian Theology," *Exchange* 49, nos. 3–4 (2020): 257–77, https://doi.org/10.1163/1572543X-12341569.

14. Philopos Anba-Bishoy, *The Flight of the Holy Family to Egypt* (Cairo: Nubar Publishing House, 1999), 7–8.

15. Al-Aref, *Tārīkh Ghazza,* 83.

16. Martin A. Meyer, *History of the City of Gaza: From the Earliest Times to the Present Day* (New York: Cambridge University Press, 1907), 57.

during his time in the Arabian Nabatean region (see Galatians 1:17).[17] While this question warrants further historical research, Gaza's deep Christian history is particularly evident in the early period of monasticism in the fourth century CE. One of the most important figures in Gaza's Christian history is St. Hilarion, born near Gaza and a companion of St. Anthony, the founding father of monasticism.[18] He is also recognized as the father of the monastic movement in Palestine. After Constantine declared Christianity the religion of the Roman Empire, following the Edict of Milan in 313 CE, Gaza gained imperial favor. The city's seaport, Maioumas, was renamed Constantia in honor of the emperor.[19]

In 393 CE, Porphyry was appointed bishop of Gaza. He gained the favor of Roman Empress Eudoxia and Emperor Arcadius and successfully obtained a decree to destroy all pagan temples in the city. One of the most significant acts was building a church on the site of Marnas temple, which he named Eudoxiana in honor of the empress. The church was consecrated in 406 CE.[20] After Porphyry's death, another church was built in his honor in 425 CE, and it was dedicated in 450 CE. In the seventh century, the Church of Eudoxiana was transformed into a mosque and renamed in honor of Caliph Omar ibn al-Khattab.[21] Nonetheless, historian Sadeq

---

17. See, N. T. Wright, "Paul, Arabia, and Elijah (Galatians 1:17)," *Journal of Biblical Literature* 115, no. 4 (1996): 683–92, https://doi.org/10.2307/3266349.

18. Hilarion was born in Thabatha, according to Sadeq, which is the modern-day valley of Gaza. See Moain Sadeq, "Christian Topography of Byzantine Gaza," *International Journal of Humanities and Social Science* 5, no. 12 (December 2015): 47–54, https://www.ancientport-santiques.com/wp-content/uploads/Documents/PLACES/Levant/Gaza-Sadeq2015.pdf.

19. Sadeq, "Christian Topography."

20. Meyer, *History of the City of Gaza,* 62 and 65.

21. Jean-Pierre Filiu, *Gaza: A History* (New York: Oxford University Press, 2014), 19.

suggests that the church may have been destroyed either during the Sassanid invasion or by the strong earthquake of 672 CE. Given that the Church of St. Porphyrius, which is located near Eudoxiana, still stands, it is more likely that the church was only partially destroyed.[22] A recollection of specific landmarks and churches in Gaza informs some of the local stories that teitas share, which will be developed in a subsequent section.

Gaza's historical prominence is further evidenced by its placement on the Madaba Mosaic Map, an ancient map of the Holy Land that goes back to the sixth century.[23] During the fifth and sixth centuries, Gaza became a center of Christian philosophy, with a school of rhetoric and with prominent figures such as Procopius and Choricius contributing to its intellectual legacy.[24] Numerous archaeological sites, such as the fourth-century Saint George Monastery in Deir Al-Balah and a church with a large mosaic dating back to 586 CE, testify to the historical Christian presence in Gaza.[25] Following the defeat of the Byzantine Empire by Muslim forces, many pagans converted to Islam, and some churches were transformed into mosques. However, Christianity in Gaza remained vibrant. The arrival of the Crusaders along the Gaza coastline brought new changes to the city and its Christian inhabitants. As previously mentioned, the Omari Mosque was briefly reconverted into a church under the Latin

---

22. Filiu, *Gaza*, 21.

23. Nathan Steinmeyer, "Madaba: The World's Oldest Holy Land Map," *Biblical Archaeology Society*, 18 February 2022, https://www.biblicalarchaeology.org/daily/biblical-artifacts/artifacts-and-the-bible/madaba-the-worlds-oldest-holy-land-map.

24. Mark the Deacon, *The Life of Porphyry*, trans. G. F. Hill (Oxford: Clarendon Press, 1913), xviii.

25. See Mahmoud Joudeh, "Al-Khader Shrine (Maqam) & the Secret within Deir al-Balah," *Rozana* (28 December 2022), https://www.rozana.ps/al-khader-shrine-maqam-the-secret-within-deir-al-balah/?lang=en.

rite, and the Crusaders replaced Greek Orthodox priests with Latin ones.[26] Yet, when Saladin's Islamic army recaptured Gaza in the early twelfth century, the balance shifted once more. During the Mamluk era, part of the Saint Porphyrius Church was transformed into Kātib al-Wilāya Mosque.[27] The transition from Mamluk to Ottoman rule did not significantly alter the status of Christians in Gaza. Christians and Muslims coexisted with relatively few conflicts, although Christians gradually became a minority. For centuries, the coastal strip remained a center of Orthodox Christianity.

In 1851, the Church Mission Society (CMS) of the Anglican Church, led by F. A. Klein, established a presence in Gaza. Reverend A. W. Shapira and his wife made significant connections with the local community, strengthening two schools for boys and girls originally established by W. D. Pritchett in 1872. In 1881, Shapira founded a medical dispensary that later became the CMS Hospital, [28] also known locally as al-Inglīzī or al-Maʿmadānī. It is the same hospital where my paternal grandfather received his training and worked as a medical laboratory technician for nearly forty years. Saint Philip's Church stands at the center of the hospital complex, which remains operational (as of November 2024), now serving as a sanctuary for Palestinians injured by Israeli attacks.[29] The Latin Catholic Church also found a home in Gaza. In 1879, an Austrian preacher established a

---

26. Meyer, *History of the City of Gaza*, 81.

27. Z. M. Shehada, "The Reflection of Interreligious Coexistence on the Cultural Morphology of the Grand Omari Mosque in Gaza," *Journal of History Culture and Art Research* 9, no. 4 (2020): 146–63.

28. Kenny Schmitt, "Rubble and Ruin: The CMS Hospital of Gaza in World War I . . . and Today?" *Contemporary Levant* (11 July 2024), doi: 10.1080/20581831.2024.2374214.

29. Dawoud Abu Alkas, "Gaza Church Opens Doors to Injured and Sick as Hospitals Fill," *Reuters*, 4 July 2024, https://www.reuters.com/world/middle-east/gaza-church-opens-doors-injured-sick-hospitals-fill-2024-07-04.

Latin Rite church, later known as the Holy Family Church,[30] further diversifying the city's Christian landscape.

During the Palestinian revolt against the British Mandate (1916–1948), Palestinian Christians in Gaza participated in the national uprising. Notably, one of the local leaders of the rebellion was a Christian, Butros Sayegh, and the intervention of Father Elias Rishawi, the leader of the Greek Orthodox community, saved Muslims convicted of participating in the revolt from being hanged.[31] In the face of British and later Zionist atrocities, Palestinian Christians in Gaza remained a resilient faith community. During the Nakba, Gaza became a refuge for displaced Palestinians from neighboring towns and villages. Many Palestinian Christians from Yaffa, Ramla, and Majdal sought refuge at the Catholic Church in the Zeitoun quarter, while the Orthodox Church of St. Porphyrius was unable to offer shelter due to a lack of financial resources.

Endangered Presence: The Struggle and Decline of Palestinian Christians in Gaza

The Nakba had a disastrous impact on the Palestinian Christian community. Many Palestinian Christian families, like my maternal teita's, were forced to flee their hometowns and seek refuge in Gaza. Between 1947 and 1949, over 750,000 Palestinians, including at least 50,000 Christians, were displaced and their towns and villages destroyed and later rebuilt and renamed.[32] Many settled in the West Bank and Gaza, holding onto the hope of returning to their homes. They dreamt of returning, a human right protected and

---

30. Filiu, *Gaza*, 31.

31. Filiu, *Gaza*, 46.

32. Bernard Sabella, "Comparing Palestinian Christians on Society and Politics: Context and Religion in Israel and Palestine," https://yplus.ps/wp-content/uploads/2021/01/Sabella-Bernard-Comparing-Palestinian-Christians-on-Society-and-Politics.pdf.

granted by the Universal Human Rights Declaration Article 13 and United Nations Resolution 194.[33] Nevertheless, Israel never allowed Palestinian refugees, including my teita and her family, to return to their hometowns.

Between 1948 and 1967, Gaza was under Egyptian civil administration. During the Six-Day War in 1967, known by Palestinians and Arabs as the Naksa, or setback, the small Christian community in Gaza found refuge in their churches as Israeli military occupation began. Despite the occupation, Palestinian Christians in Gaza remained actively involved in community-building initiatives and resistance movements.[34] There are currently four Christian schools in Gaza that serve the local community: two Catholic, one Orthodox, and one Evangelical.[35] Between 1994 and 2000, Gaza's Christian community flourished, with annual Christmas celebrations attended by both Muslims and Christians.

The story of Palestinian Christians in Gaza is a microcosm of the broader Palestinian struggle. Over the decades, Gaza's Christian community continued to face forced displacement. The declining population of Palestinian Christians in historical Palestine is alarming, and in Gaza, the situation is even more severe.[36] In 1847, French diplomats

---

33. United Nations, "Universal Declaration of Human Rights," https://www.un.org/en/about-us/universal-declaration-of-human-rights#:~:text=Article%2013,to%20return%20to%20his%20country; United Nations, "The Right of Return of the Palestinian People," New York, 1978, https://www.un.org/unispal/document/auto-insert-210170/

34. Filiu, *Gaza*, 155.

35. George Akroush, *Mapping of Christian Organizations in Palestine: Social and Economic Impact* (Bethlehem: Diyar Publications, 2021), https://www.daralkalima.edu.ps/uploads/files/Mapping%20of%20Christian%20Organizations%204Final.pdf.

36. "Christian Presence in Gaza at Risk of Disappearing," *International Christian Concern*, https://www.persecution.org/2024/05/01/christian-prescence-in-gaza-at-risk-of-disappearing/#:~:text=For%20now%2C%20many%20are%20deciding,is%20not%20an%20easy%20one; Simon Caldwell, "Christian Community in Gaza under 'Real' Risk

estimated Gaza's population at 40,000 Muslims and 500 Christians.[37] By 1884–85, the Ottoman census reported 877 Christians in Gaza. This number grew to 1,058 by 1911–12 and fluctuated throughout the British Mandate, peaking at 1,300 by 1946.[38] Following the Israeli occupation, the 1967 census recorded 2,305 Christians in Gaza,[39] which increased to 2,543 by 1990.[40] However, by 1997, the population had fallen to 1,688, and further declined to 1,313 by 2014.[41]

Since the Israeli blockade of Gaza in 2007, Gazan Christians have suffered the same hardships as their Muslim neighbors, including the lack of clean water, food shortages, limited electricity and fuel, and inadequate health care.[42] In

---

of Complete 'Disappearance,'" *Catholic Herald*, June 29, 2024, https://catholicherald.co.uk/christian-community-in-gaza-under-real-risk-of-complete-disappearance/; "Palestinian Christians—The Forcible Displacement and Dispossession Continues," *Badil and Kairos Palestine*, May 2023, https://www.kairospalestine.ps/images/kairos-badil-2023.pdf.

37. Justin McCarthy, *The Population of Palestine: Population History and Statistics of the Late Ottoman Period and the Mandate* (New York: Cambridge University Press, 1990), 30.

38. McCarthy, *The Population of Palestine*, 50–69. Numbers vary depending on various factors or documents. Nevertheless, the variation is not significant, as McCarthy demonstrates in his book.

39. "The 1967 Census of the West Bank and Gaza Strip: A Digitized Version," *Levy Economics Institute of Bard College*, https://www.levyinstitute.org/palestinian-census.

40. Wael R. Ennab, "Population and Demographic Developments in the West Bank and Gaza Strip until 1990," *United Nations Conference for Trade and Development*, 28 June 1994, https://unctad.org/system/files/official-document/poecdcseud1.en.pdf.

41. "Survey of the Christian Community in the Gaza Strip," *Young Men's Christian Association*, May 2014, https://www.researchgate.net/publication/283330789_SURVEY_OF_THE_CHRISTIAN_COMMUNITY_IN_THE_GAZA_STRIP.

42. See, for example, "Suffocation and Isolation: 17 Years of Israeli Blockade on Gaza," *Euro-Med Monitor*, https://euromedmonitor.org/en/gaza; "Israel: Unlawful Gaza Blockade Deadly for Children," *Human Rights Watch*, October 18, 2023, https://www.hrw.org/news/2023/10/18/israel-unlawful-gaza-blockade-deadly-children/.

addition, there are severe restrictions on movement from Gaza to the West Bank and Jerusalem, even for religious worship. The Israeli permit regime frequently denies Palestinian Christians permits to travel to hospitals in the West Bank or Jerusalem, as well as to visit holy sites in Bethlehem and Jerusalem.[43] The ongoing siege and blockade of Gaza have also meant that Gazan Orthodox Christians are denied a significant tradition in Orthodox Christianity—access to the Holy Light, عيد النور ʿĪd al-Nūr, which emanates from Jesus's tomb in the Church of the Holy Sepulchre in Jerusalem and symbolizes the resurrection of Christ.

The ongoing genocide against Gaza since October 7, 2023, has been catastrophic for Gazan Christians.[44] At least sixteen people have been killed in an Israeli airstrike that resulted in the collapse of a building within the St. Porphyrius Church's vicinity on October 19, 2023,[45] including two women near the Holy Family Catholic Church[46] and an elderly woman

---

43. See Kenny Schmitt, "Gazan Christians: Pilgrimage Permits, Migration, and the Exchange of Precarity," *Exchange* 49, no. 3/4 (2020): 316–38, https://doi.org/10.1163/1572543X-12341572.

44. The term "genocide" in describing the Israeli war on Gaza has been a subject of controversy. Nevertheless, many human rights groups and organizations have argued thoroughly in favor of using the concept of genocide. See "Genocide in Gaza: Analysis of International Law and Its Application to Israel's Military Actions since October 7, 2023," *University Network for Human Rights*, May 15, 2024, https://www.humanrightsnetwork.org/genocide-in-gaza#:~:text=After%20review ing%20the%20facts%20established,2023%2C%20violate%20the%20 Genocide%20Convention.

45. Karen Zraick and Ameera Harouda, "Israel Airstrike Hits Gaza City," *New York Times*, October 20, 2023, https://www.nytimes.com/2023/10/20/world/middleeast/israel-airstrike-gaza-city.html; Nidal Al-Mughrabi, "Orthodox Church Says It Was Hit by Israeli Air Strike in Gaza," *Reuters*, October 20, 2023, https://www.reuters.com/world/orthodox-church-says-it-was-hit-by-israeli-air-strike-gaza-2023-10-20.

46. "In Gaza, Israelis Attack Holy Family Parish; Two Women Killed," *Vatican News*, December 1, 2023, https://www.vaticannews.

shot by an Israeli sniper.[47] Many others have succumbed to medical complications due to a lack of access to health care. The destruction of church properties and homes belonging to Christian families adds to the tragedy. Some people try to link the violence to the attacks of October 7, 2023, but this perspective overlooks decades of Israeli settler colonialism and the expulsion of Palestinians.[48] The real genocide and ethnic cleansing of Palestinians, including Christians, has been brewing in the minds of Western Christians long before 2023 or even 1948.

As of November 2024, fewer than 650 Christians remain in Gaza, most sheltering at St. Porphyrius Greek Orthodox Church or at Holy Family Church.[49] These numbers underscore the significant decline of Palestinian Christians in Gaza. In a recent message during Easter, Archbishop Alexius of St. Porphyrius Church expressed his fear that the church will soon be emptied of its congregants due to the ongoing genocide.

Zionism and the Plight of Palestinian Christians in Gaza

The desire to ethically cleanse Palestine, and Gaza, predates Jewish Zionism, as many Western Christian leaders have

---

va/en/world/news/2023-12/in-gaza-israelis-attack-holy-family-parish-two-women-killed.html.

47. Nadda Osman, "Christian Music Teacher Killed in Gaza as Israel-Palestine War Rages," *Middle East Eye*, November 14, 2023, https://www.middleeasteye.net/news/israel-palestine-war-christian-music-teacher-killed-gaza.

48. See, for example, Rashid Khalidi, *The Hundred Years' War on Palestine: A History of Settler Colonial Conquest and Resistance, 1917–2017* (New York: Metropolitan Books, 2020).

49. A Palestinian Christian in Gaza testifies that about 640 Christians remain in Gaza as of October 2024. See Bethlehem Bible College, "Gaza's Christians in the Face of War," 27 September 2024, https://bethbc.edu/blog/2024/09/27/gazas-christians-in-the-face-of-war.

long nurtured a proto-Zionist ideology.[50] They supported the colonization of Palestine and transferring land to European Jews at the expense of the Palestinian indigenous population. To push this agenda, they propagated the idea that Palestine was a "deserted land," or *terra nullius*. Take Keith Alexander, a Scottish clergyman in 1846, for example. He, along with Lord Shaftesbury, who was the president of the London Society for Promoting Christianity among the Jews, claimed that Palestine was "a country without people"[51] and "a country without a nation."[52] They completely overlooked the fact that Palestine was home to a vibrant society with a rich history, including a Palestinian Christian community that was full of teitas.

The historical context and the numbers speak for themselves, exposing the lies perpetuated by Europeans. Settler colonization of the land between the Jordan River and the Mediterranean Sea—wrapped in a religious guise—grew out of a European interest in colonizing Palestine and hastening the end times.[53] Lord Shaftesbury played a focal role in shaping the Anglican Church in England and lobbying for his ideas. As Rosemary Radford Ruether points out, he was instrumental in these developments.[54] Despite his death

---

50. On the origins of Christian Zionism as a proto-Zionist ideology, see Robert O. Smith, *More Desired Than Our Owne Salvation* (Oxford: Oxford University Press, 2013).

51. Gershon Shafir, "Theorizing Zionist Settler Colonialism in Palestine," in *The Routledge Handbook of the History of Settler Colonialism*, ed. Edward Cavanagh and Lorenzo Veracini (Oxford: Routledge, 2017), 339–52 (339).

52. Edwin Hodder, *The Life and Work of the Seventh Earl of Shaftesbury, K.G.* (London: Cassell & Co., 1887), 493. See also Mitri Raheb, "Palestinian Christian Reflections on Christian Zionism," in *Comprehending Christian Zionism: Perspectives in Comparison*, ed. Göran Gunner and Robert O. Smith (Minneapolis: Fortress Press, 2014), 191–98 (192).

53. Raheb, "Palestinian Christian Reflections," 192.

54. Rosemary Radford Ruether, "Christian Zionism and Mainline Western Christian Churches," in *Comprehending Christian Zionism: Per-*

in 1885, Lord Shaftesbury's vision continued to shape the Church of England and influence the imperial politics of the British Empire, ultimately leading to the 1917 Balfour Declaration, which promised Palestine to Zionism.[55]

Western Christian support for the Zionist settler-colonial project never waned. For some Western Christians, especially Evangelicals, the establishment of the settler-colonial regime in 1948 was seen as the fulfillment of biblical prophecies.[56] This perspective conveniently ignores the suffering of Palestinian Christians who were dispossessed of their land. While Gaza was not directly colonized in 1948, its residents still faced the fallout. Over two decades later, in 1967, the Israeli military occupied Gaza, along with the West Bank, Jerusalem, Sinai, and the Golan Heights. According to Mitri Raheb, a notable Palestinian theologian and Lutheran pastor, the Israeli victory was seen as a divine miracle, in which "David the Jew" triumphed over "Goliath Arabs," boosting Jewish and Christian messianism.[57]

It is crucial to note that both Jewish and Christian Zionism weaponized the Bible against the Palestinian people. For Palestinian Christians, the Holy Bible, which they celebrate as a collection of their ancestors' faith stories, has become a tool for justifying their forceful displacement. Cedar Duaybis, a Palestinian educator and cofounder of the Sabeel Center for Liberation Theology, describes this dilemma as a "faith

spectives in Comparison, ed. Göran Gunner and Robert O. Smith (Minneapolis: Fortress Press, 2014), 179–90 (181).

55. Radford Ruether, "Christian Zionism," 182.

56. A LifeWay poll shows that 80 percent of Evangelicals in America believe that Israel is a fulfillment of biblical prophecy. See Philip Bump, "Half of Evangelicals Support Israel because They Believe It Is Important for Fulfilling End Times Prophecy," *Washington Post*, May 14, 2018, https://www.washingtonpost.com/news/politics/wp/ 2018/ 05/14/half-of-evangelicals-support-israel-because-they-believe-it-is-important-for-fulfilling-end-times-prophecy/.

57. Raheb, "Palestinian Christian Reflections," 194–95.

Nakba," a catastrophe that uprooted their theological foundations and left them feeling utterly lost.[58] Palestinian Christians did not just lose their homes; they felt that they lost their Bible, too. They faced the dual challenge of seeking liberation for their land and their faith. Since the onset of the Israeli genocide in Gaza, certain Christian groups—whether knowingly or not—continue to provide ideological cover, theological justification, and financial support for the Israeli settler-colonial war.[59] Zionist Christians in the United States, particularly through organizations like Christians United for Israel (CUFI), have become a significant political force supporting the Israeli government.[60] As in the nineteenth century, these Zionist Christians often overlook the humanitarian crisis facing Palestinians in Gaza, including those who share their faith. Even worse, they seem complicit in it. The unwavering support that Zionist Christians and Evangelicals offer to Israeli settler colonialism has contributed to the near extinction of Palestinian Christians.

Faith and Faithfulness of Palestinian Christian Grandmothers

Palestinian women and grandmothers have been playing a significant role in the oral transmission of Palestinian his-

58. Cedar Duaybis, "The Three-Fold Nakba," *Cornerstone* 66 (2013): 8–9. See also Ateek, *A Palestinian Theology of Liberation* (Maryknoll, NY: Orbis Books, 2017), 28.

59. Melanie Lidman, "Evangelical Christians Continue to Take Volunteer Trips to Israel," *Associated Press*, updated March 13, 2024, https://apnews.com/article/evangelical-christians-israel-volunteer-trips-462329e04459191fd6ae061e722cae30.

60. Abigail Hauslohner, "Evangelicals' Support for Israel Stirs Controversy amid Gaza Conflict," *Washington Post*, April 13, 2024, https://www.washingtonpost.com/national-security/2024/04/13/evangelicals-israel-gaza-republicans/.

tory.[61] Teitas are organic storytellers, and their stories are filled with testimonies of a life committed to the teachings of Christ. My grandmothers, my teitas, were my primary educators on the history of our land and faith.

A Beautiful Grace: The Stories of Teitas

Teita Naima, which means Grace, is my paternal grandmother, a nurturing figure who served as a grandmother to many. Known for her kindness, she wet-nursed numerous babies from her neighbors and relatives, caring for her own grandchildren as well as those of her community. Her deep knowledge of the stories and history of Gaza has left a lasting impact on me. One of the tales she shared, which was later confirmed by an older Muslim taxi driver, recounts an event during the Muslim army's conquest of Gaza. According to this story, upon seizing control of the city, the Muslim forces transformed the Church of Eudoxiana into a mosque. They approached the sanctuary and attempted to open the artoforion, the tabernacle that contained the reserved Eucharist. Suddenly, a stream of blood began flowing from it, covering the floor. As Naima and the taxi driver recounted, the blood reached up to their knees. While this may have been an exaggeration, it underscores the sacredness and significance of the story. In a desperate attempt to understand the phenomenon, the Muslims brought imams to pray and even magicians to perform rituals, but none could halt the mysterious flow. Eventually, Orthodox priests were summoned, and as they began to recite the liturgy, the blood returned to the artoforion.

---

61. See Rosemary Sayigh, "Palestinian Camp Women as Tellers of History," *Journal of Palestine Studies* 27, no. 2 (Winter 1998): 42–58; Rosemary Sayigh, "The Nakba and Oral History," Lecture at Issam Fares Institute for Public Policy and International Affairs, 10 May 2018, https://www.palestine-studies.org/en/node/1636005.

This tale both highlights the spiritual weight of the site and reflects the deep interconnections between the communities of Gaza throughout history. I recall countless visits to the mosque, where I would observe the northern gate still bearing remnants of the original stone, intricately carved with the bread of the Eucharist. Adjacent to the mosque is the old market, bustling with jewelry stores, which further enriches the tapestry of life in Gaza. Beyond the personal narratives, Gaza has a rich and complex Christian history. The city has served as a vital center for Christian thought and culture since antiquity, contributing to the development of early Christianity. It was home to significant theological figures and played a crucial role in the spread of Christian beliefs throughout the region. Today, the stories of both Naima and Gaza continue to resonate, intertwining the personal with the historical, and emphasizing the enduring legacy of faith and community in this storied land.

Teita Jamila, which means Beautiful, is my maternal grandmother. She embodies the plight of countless Palestinians who have experienced displacement since 1948. At just nine years old, during the Nakba, she faced the horrors of being uprooted. Living in Yaffa's al-Ajami neighborhood as a third-grade student, she and her family were forced to flee amid the Zionist militant attacks that aimed to ethnically cleanse Palestinian villages and towns. Her stepmother, Marthe, fled with her four stepchildren and child, unable to wait for Jamila's father, Hanna, to return from working in an orange grove. They took whatever valuables they could carry and boarded a truck with other fleeing families heading to Gaza. Hanna followed soon after, finding refuge at the Holy Family Catholic Church, where they lived in a tent for several months. Believing the war would soon end and they could return home, Hanna secured a job at a soap factory owned by the al-Tawīl family. Many refugees settled in what became al-Shati' Refugee Camp. Some Christian families were offered land to build houses, but Hanna firmly rejected this option, clinging to the dream of returning to Yaffa. Others moved to Christian Camp (Mukhayyam, al-Masīḥiyya), at the end of al-Wīhda Street, yet none abandoned the hope of returning to their homeland. Hanna died in the 1980s, and Jamila never returned to Yaffa. Nevertheless, Jamila neither grew bitter nor desired revenge. One of her sons married an American Jew who had family in Palestine, and Jamila seemed to understand that Zionism and Judaism are not synonymous. She distinguished that the pain and trauma of her displacement was because of Zionism, an ideology to which her daughter-in-law did not adhere. Jamila's family has become a challenge to narratives that assume that Jews and Palestinians are eternal enemies and that Zionism and Judaism are one and the same.

Grandmothers as Faith Anchors

Grandmothers have been anchors of faith and wisdom to generations throughout history and across nations. In Palestine, teitas represent the long-standing connectedness to family, homeland, and faith. Within the Palestinian Christian community, they have been teachers of faith and the Bible, exemplifying faithfulness to Christ's teachings amidst hardship. Armas beautifully states that grandmothers "are the functional priestesses and theologians" in their families.[62] Although teitas were often formally undereducated, like my grandmothers who barely finished middle school, their faith and life experiences made them priestesses and theologians for generations of Palestinian Christians. Armas asserts that "our abuelitas may be 'uneducated' by the dominant culture's standards, but they possess PhDs in prayer and Bible interpretation. They may not be ordained as official priests or pastors, but they've been playing those roles behind the scenes

---

62. Armas, *Abuelita Faith*, 19.

forever, noticed and called by God."[63] Armas also discusses
the role of grandmother figures in indigenous civilizations and
in the lives of figures like the apostle Paul and Martin Luther
King Jr., recognizing how abuelita theologies arise from marginalized women's unique contexts and experiences. "I like to
think of not one abuelita theology but multiple abuelita theologies," she writes, "born from the diversity that makes up
the lived experiences of marginalized women across religious
expressions, races, ethnicities, cultures, classes, and places."[64]
In what follows, I wish to introduce three principles of a
Palestinian abuelita theology, or Teita's Faith.

Rooted in the Past of Our Great-Grandmother

Teita's faith draws inspiration from female heroines of
faith, most importantly, Virgin Mary. For many Palestinian
Christian—and Muslim—women, Mary, or مريم (Mariam), is
regarded as their great grandmother. She is a role model to
follow for obedience to God and faith that God's will shall
always prevail. It is common for Palestinian women to refer
to her as "Teita Mariam" or "Setna Mariam," with Setna being
synonymous with Teita. Mary exemplifies meekness and
faithfulness. In her Magnificat (Luke 1:46–55), she expresses
profound wisdom and understanding of God's movements in
history to bring liberation and redemption to those oppressed
by the Empire. The Magnificat teaches us that Empire will ultimately cease, as God acts to humble the prideful and uplift the
meek. Palestinian theologians, following the tradition of liberation theology, have extensively explored how Mary's song
challenges imperial power.[65] Like their great-grandmother,

---

63. Armas, *Abuelita Faith*, 19.

64. Armas, *Abuelita Faith*.

65. See, for example, Rafiq Khoury's *Toward Incarnational Theology*
(2012), which is published in Arabic, *Naḥw Lāhūt Mutajassid fi Turbat
Bilādinā, Min Ajl Ḥudūd Maftūḥa Bayn al-Zaman wa-al-Abadiyya* (Beit
Jala: Al-Liqa' Center, 2012), 39.

teitas were convinced and had faith that God would intervene once again in history to bring about justice and liberation from the imperial oppression of Zionism and Israel.

Faithfulness by Words and Deeds

Teita's faith exemplifies faithfulness to Jesus's teaching of loving one's neighbor. It encompasses both the orthodoxy and orthopraxy of the Christian faith. For teitas, the practical method of loving neighbors involves transcending religious prejudice and fostering a shared life.[66] They modeled this spirit of togetherness by sharing food with their Muslim neighbors. There was no fear of one another, nor did discussions of faith become divisive. Instead, they shared a common language, history, and struggle against colonial oppression. For Naima, loving her neighbor manifested in the intimate act of wet-nursing her Muslim neighbors' babies. Sharing special dishes, such as Burbara, Rumania (an essential dish in Gaza Christian cuisine, during Orthodox Lent, made with fresh pomegranate or molasses), also symbolized love and unity. To my grandmother, liberated from the greed of capitalism and colonial expansion, her pomegranate, olive, and lemon trees were sacred gifts from God, meant to be shared freely with her neighbors.

Language of Love Is Resistance and Resilience

Teita's faith embraces Jesus's teachings of loving our enemies and nonviolent resistance. Palestinian Christians actively participate in the resistance movement against Israeli settler colonialism, with the vast majority choosing the path

---

66. Palestinian theologian and clergy Rafiq Khoury prefers also the concept of making or building life together rather than co-existence. See Rafiq Khoury, "Palestinian Contextual Theology: A General Survey," in *Christian Theology in the Palestinian Context*, ed. Rafiq Khoury and Rainer Zimmer-Winkel (Berlin: AphorismA Verlag, 2019), 9–48 (14).

of nonviolence. They confronted and continue to confront their aggressors with the language and logic of love.[67] Jesus's teaching to "love your enemy" (Matthew 5:43–44) was frequently emphasized in the churches and Christian organizations of my youth. It was not viewed as a command for surrender or passivity but as an active commitment to justice through nonviolent means. Teita Naima exemplified this love.

One afternoon, during the First Intifada (1987–1993), an Israeli military unit invaded our home in the old city of Gaza, searching for young men accused of throwing stones. While I, a terrified seven-year-old, watched, Naima calmly sat on the floor, baking bread. As the soldiers prepared to leave, she suddenly shouted at one of them, handing him a warm loaf and urging him to share it with the others. I was bewildered — why would she feed them?

Later, as I grew in my faith and understanding of what it means to be a Christian, I realized Naima was faithfully following Jesus's command to love one's enemy (Matthew 5:44) and Paul's teaching to feed one's enemy (Romans 12:20; Proverbs 25:21–23). Naima chose faithfulness over resentment, embodying a logic of resistance grounded in love. Her act of kindness disarmed and challenged the power dynamics at play. Rather than bitterness or anger, Naima, like her Lord, extended bread even to those who intended harm to her family. Paul's teaching in 1 Corinthians 11:23–29 became even more vivid in that moment; the broken bread symbolized God's reconciliation, while Naima's bread served as an invitation to repentance and transformation. In a similar

67. Resistance with the "logic of love" is an integral part of Palestinian Christian theology as emphasized by the ecumenical document of Kairos Palestine (4.2.3, 4.2.5). See Kairos Palestine, *A Moment of Truth: A Word of Faith, Hope and Love from the Heart of Palestinian Suffering* (Bethlehem, 2009), https://www.kairospalestine.ps/index.php/about-kairos/kairos-palestine-document.

manner, Jamila refused to let bitterness against Zionist Jews consume her. She did not allow the devastation of Nakba to fracture her family. Instead, Jamila and her family became a living example of healing and inclusion. Through her faith in Christ, who heals and reconciles, her family embodies Paul's teaching on the mystery of Christ, which unites all people (Galatians 3:28).

Teita's Faith demonstrates a deep and unwavering commitment to the teachings of Christ, rejecting passivity, hatred, and fear. They were rooted in their love for their Lord and their land. Their orthopraxy provides a powerful model of faith in action—faith that inspires action and action that is fueled by faith.

Conclusion

Teitas are more than storytellers in the faith. They are exemplars of faith. Their unwavering love for their Lord, their land, their neighbors, and even their enemies embodies a Christlike life that aspires to bring justice, peace, and reconciliation. This chapter has explored the history and resilient faith of Palestinian Christians in Gaza through the brief narratives of two teitas. While these stories inspire, they are also deeply agonizing, marked by oppression, displacement, and acts of genocide perpetrated in the name of God by Christian and Jewish Zionists. Despite these hardships, teitas and the broader Palestinian Christian community in Gaza and Palestine exemplify a faithful witness to Christ and resilience in their ancestral land. They live in trust, echoing the faith of Great-Grandmother Mary: God will ultimately bring justice and liberation to the oppressed.

2

Guatemala and Gaza

Enfleshed Divinity in Women's Ethics of Care

MARAH SARJI
Nazareth

But, Gaza,
nothing will turn back
dismembered body parts
to whole bodies again.

No peace could ever
make up for a single funeral
of the many
that never had the chance
to honor a single whole body.
　　　　—Yahya Ashour[1]

Informed by the lives and practices of Palestinian women in Gaza and Mayan women in Guatemala, this chapter attempts to provide an answer to the question "Wenak ya Allah?"—Where are you, God, amid genocide? I advocate for an approach that embraces women's experiences as sources for reflection and inspection of our theologies. Following George Khodr's theology of the cross, I explore the

---

1. Yahya Ashour, *A Gaza of Siege and Genocide*, 3–4, https://mizna.org/product/a-gaza-of-siege-and-genocide.

parallels between the Guatemalan and Palestinian contexts. I argue, following Guatemalan and Palestinian women's embodiment of care, that the commitment to ethics of care embodies God's presence within the community in Gaza and Guatemala. We see God embodied in those who practice care, particularly women.

Despite all, women and men in militarized zones navigate death-dealing circumstances daily, while fighting for their well-being and that of their loved ones. Although women's bodies bear witness to the colonial sexual violence, no major work in Palestinian theology thus far has taken up women's lives and concerns as primary resources for ethical and theological reflection.[2] By centering the body, I reaffirm that human bodies, inseparable from our souls, were created in God's image. The body represents power, and state powers act against the body, attempting to define the boundaries of nationhood and assert sovereignty over it.[3] Within a militarized context, notably during genocide, bodies are "not simply a metaphor but a political reality."[4]

I develop my discussion following a solidarity delegation I participated in in May 2024, which focused on the aftermath of genocides and state-terror in Guatemala. This chapter aims to learn from the materially interconnected contexts of Guatemala and Palestine, where the same forces facilitating genocide in Gaza, namely, the United States and the State of Israel, were active actors in the genocide of two hundred

---

2. Although Jean Zaru's book *Occupied with Nonviolence: A Palestinian Woman Speaks* (Minneapolis: Fortress Press, 2008) reflects an embodied theology and commitment to active nonviolent work for peace, it does little to develop theological reflections informed by her lived experiences as a leader with multiple identities.

3. Giorgio Agamben, *Homo Sacer: Sovereign Power and Bare Life* (Meridian; Stanford, CA: Stanford University Press, 1998), 6.

4. Nadira Shalhoub-Kevorkian, *Militarization and Violence against Women in Conflict Zones in the Middle East: A Palestinian Case-Study* (Cambridge: Cambridge University Press, 2009), 148.

thousand Guatemalans, predominantly indigenous Mayan peoples, from the late 1960s until the early 1990s.

I first discuss the interconnectedness of Guatemala's and Gaza's genocides. Then, I discuss the invisible experiences of women. Lastly, I attempt to answer the question "Wenak ya Allah?" through centering the practices and ethics of care embodied by Guatemalan and Gazan women.

Guatemala as Antecedent to Gaza

Guatemala's connection to Palestine is not merely metaphorical. It is deeply rooted in tangible material and imperial structures. The oppression and genocide of Mayans in Guatemala from 1954 to 1996 began with a U.S.-orchestrated military coup.[5] It was sustained by continuous supplies of arms and services from Israel.[6] Although Israel was Guatemala's primary supplier for arms in certain periods, its advisory role was more significant, with direct involvement in training police and military troops,[7] including "assistance in electronic surveillance systems, intelligence gathering, and military-agricultural resettlement projects in former rebel areas."[8]

---

5. The colonial legacy of the 1524 Spanish conquest of Guatemala endures in the institutionalization of de-development and impoverishment, notably in resource exportation industries. For more, see Susanne Jonas and Harry E. Vanden, "Guatemala," in *Politics of Latin America: The Power Game*, 5th ed. (New York: Oxford University Press, 2015), 571–605; Catherine Nolin and Grahame Russell, *Testimonio: Canadian Mining in the Aftermath of Genocides in Guatemala*, 1st ed. (Toronto: Between the Lines, 2021).

6. Bishara Bahbah, "Israel and Latin America," in *Israel and Latin America: The Military Connection* (New York: Springer, 1986), 59–109; Gabriel Schivone, "Israel's Shadowy Role in Guatemala's Dirty War," in *The Electronic Intifada*, January 20, 2017, https://electronicintifada.net/content/israels-shadowy-role-guatemalas-dirty-war/19286.

7. Bahbah, *Israel and Latin America*, 160–61.

8. Bahbah, *Israel and Latin America*, 161.

A stark example of this connection is Israeli involvement in the rule of General Efraín Ríos Montt, one of the most brutal genocidal tyrants in Guatemala's history, backed by the United States and trained at the U.S. Army School of the Americas.[9] An Evangelical Christian, Ríos Montt "thanked his God in heaven for anointing him as Guatemala's president, but on earth he thanked Israel for establishing his March 1982 military coup."[10] Six weeks after assuming power, Montt declared the highlands strict military zones and initiated a scorched-earth campaign that included brutal massacres, effectively obliterating "not only . . . homes and possessions, but the very landscape of place and belonging."[11]

During Montt's reign, Israel assisted in training and advising the Guatemalan military in counterinsurgency tactics aimed at subduing the popular Mayan-supported resistance guerrillas and enforcing sustained pacification.[12] From 1981 until 1983 alone, "440 villages were entirely wiped off the map, and up to 150,000 civilians were killed or disappeared," with over one million internally displaced people

---

9. The School of America's curriculum trained various Latin American military officers in "sniper training, commando and psychological warfare, military intelligence, and interrogation tactics." These officers took part in brutal human rights abuses and assumed positions as dictators in the region. See Linda Panetta and Randy Serraglio, "Training Assassins," *NACLA Report on the Americas*, December 2000, 28, 202672629, ProQuest Central; Social Science Premium Collection.

10. Gabriel Schivone, "Israel's Proxy War in Guatemala," *North American Congress on Latin America* (April 23, 2013), https://nacla.org/news/2013/4/23/israel%E2%80%99s-proxy-war-guatemala.

11. Virginia Garrard-Burnett, *Terror in the Land of the Holy Spirit: Guatemala under General Efrain Rios Montt, 1982–1983* (New York: Oxford University Press, 2009), 97.

12. To read more on the "Fusiles y Frijoles" systematic campaign for obliterating the Mayan-supported guerrilla resistance, establishment of civil patrols, and villages following the "kibbutz" archetype in Israel, see Garrard-Burnett, *Terror in the Land,* 53–112; Bahbah, "Israel and Latin America," 164.

and 200,000 refugees in Mexico.[13] This involvement effectively assisted "every facet of attack on the Guatemalan people."[14] Some Guatemalan military leaders even referred to the "Palestinization" of the indigenous Mayan population.[15] The practices of the economic-military elites in Guatemala are in direct relation to Palestine. In a global economy dominated by settler-colonial states, local issues are linked to global policies and interests.[16] The "US and Israel [are] partners in genocide" in both contexts through funding, manufacturing, and providing weaponry, and impunity on the world stage.[17]

Effectively, "the massacres, scorched earth operations, forced disappearances and executions of Mayan authorities, leaders and spiritual guides, were not only an attempt to destroy the social base of the guerrillas, but above all, to destroy the cultural values that ensured cohesion and collective action in Mayan communities."[18] While Montt favored massacres over forced disappearances as a counterinsurgency tactic, both worked in tandem to subjugate and exterminate the resistance in Guatemala.

The Invisible Experiences of Women during Genocide

Wearing her traje and carrying the anguish of loss and abuse, Rosalina Tuyuc, a survivor of Ríos Montt's genocidal campaign and cofounder of the National Association of

---

13. Jonas and Vanden, "Guatemala," 580.

14. Schivone, "Israel's Proxy War in Guatemala."

15. Bahbah, "Israel and Latin America," 164.

16. Nolin and Russell, *Testimonio*, 7.

17. Mark Taylor, "Israel and Genocide: Not Only in Gaza," *New Age*, December 23, 2023, sec. Opinion, https://www.newagebd.net/article/220889/israel-and-genocide-not-only-in-gaza.

18. United Nations, "Guatemala, Memory of Silence: Tzínil Naʼtabál: Report of the Commission for Historical Clarification: Conclusions and Recommendations" (S.l: The Commission, 1998), 23.

Guatemalan Widows (CONAVIGUA), shared her personal story and the broader struggle for truth and justice led by women.[19] During "the violence" period, from the 1970s until the mid-1980s, Rosalina led a communal cooperative in San Juan Comalapa, a Mayan community targeted by the government and military under the accusation of "communism." After being targeted personally for her leadership, she went into hiding in the early 1980s. The military forces in June 1982 kidnapped her father instead. Three years later, her husband and brother-in-law likewise were forcibly disappeared and executed. Many families suffered from the same violence. The military initially targeted men through forced disappearances, tortures, and executions. Then, they targeted women and young girls with systematic sexual violence perpetrated by military and death squads. Through the scorched-earth campaign, Montt's military devastated the region, burning and destroying it, and prohibiting the residents from returning.

Today, Rosalina reports, an estimated sixty thousand women in Guatemala suffer from the trauma and disease contracted from rape, with no justice being served. Rape has been a particularly devastating counterinsurgency tactic, severely impacting the Mayan social fabric and causing lasting harm to the community. In Guatemala, the exertion of power over bodies was systematically carried out through sexual harassment and rape of women and children, both during massacres and state-sanctioned capture.

Rape was more than just individual misconduct. It was a calculated counterinsurgency strategy. On the one hand, participation in rape served to build comradeship, control troops, and boost morale. On the other hand, violence

19. To read more on Rosalina Tuyuc's story and activism, visit https://interactive.unwomen.org/multimedia/feature/generation equalityrising/es/rosalina.html.

against women created multidimensional fear of the regime, of sexual violence, and of "defilement and subsequent public disrepute" in a patriarchal culture that upholds female purity.[20]

Targeting indigenous women, who are highly valued as cultural reproducers in Guatemalan families, effectively subdued these communities. Rape, intended to strip women of their dignity and honor, left survivors burdened with shame, alienation, and the need to face the aftermath in secrecy. The moral costs of rape were higher in a patriarchal society, exacerbating the trauma. However, Hastings argues that silence over political rape does not necessarily stem from cultural and internal patriarchal factors, but from "national and international systems of justice."[21]

Sexual assault of women and forced disappearances of men disrupted family ties and the social fabric, harming women's identities and roles as primary caregivers in Mayan communities. Historically, Mayan women have been the primary caregivers and sustainers of the family's well-being and its status as a social unit.[22] The prolonged uncertainty over the fate of relatives hindered women's abilities to regain their roles and attitudes toward caregiving to their communities.[23]

---

20. M. Gabriela Torres, "Bloody Deeds/Hechos Sangrientos, Reading Guatemala's Record of Political Violence in Cadaver Reports," in *When States Kill: Latin America, the U.S., and Technologies of Terror*, 1st ed. (Austin: University of Texas Press, 2005), 158–59.

21. Julie A. Hastings, "Silencing State-Sponsored Rape in and beyond a Transnational Guatemalan Community," *Violence Against Women* 8, no. 10 (2002): 1158, doi:10.1177/107780120200801002.

22. Cathy Blacklock, "Democratization and Popular Women's Organizations," in *Journeys of Fear*, ed. Lisa L. North and Alan B. Simmons (Refugee Return and National Transformation in Guatemala; Montreal: McGill-Queen's University Press, 1999), 198, http://www.jstor.org.ezproxy.princeton.edu/stable/j.ctt80t2h.15.

23. Blacklock, "Democratization and Popular Women's Organizations," 199.

While visiting other organizations and sights of struggle in Guatemala, it was clear to me that, similar to Rosalina, many women have joined social movements to rebuild Mayan life and preserve historical memory and justice. Such movements include the Association of Relatives of the Detained and Disappeared of Guatemala (FAMDEGUA),[24] in partnership with the Forensic Anthropology Foundation of Guatemala (FAFG).[25] Participation in these movements gives the women hopes for restoring the remnants of their relatives, the offering of a dignified burial, and seeking justice through the legal system for the crimes against humanity committed. Furthermore, various women have been leading organizations and communal struggles against present efforts for their displacement across the country. Despite all forces and locations of victimhood, Guatemalan women have shown resilience and resolve to care for their communities' health, well-being, and cohesion.

The humanitarian crisis in Gaza, much like Guatemala, is man-made, in which the Israeli economic and military elites play the central role.[26] Said Shehadeh, writing after the 2014 assault on Gaza, proposes that Gaza is a massive "torture chamber."[27] The repeated violence against Palestinians in Gaza is an integral part of the "ongoing policy to subjugate, subdue, silence, and erase Palestinians."[28] Shehadeh identifies a paradigm shift in the settler-colonial regime's approach since 2014 "from managing and controlling the resistance [in

---

24. Learn more here: https://pbi-guatemala.org/en/who-we-accompany-gt/fam degua.

25. Learn more here: https://fafg.org/en.

26. Helga Tawil-Souri and Dina Matar, eds., *Gaza as Metaphor* (London: C. Hurst & Co., 2016).

27. Said Shehadeh, "Ghazeh El Sumud: Confronting Israeli Mass Torture," in *Gaza as Meraphor*, ed. Helga Tawil-Souri and Dina Matar (London: C. Hurst & Co., 2016), 51.

28. Shehadeh, "Ghazeh El Sumud," 47.

Gaza], to attempts at destroying it psychologically—mainly by breaking the Palestinian psyche and the social fabric from which it draws its resilience."[29]

Through policies of mass torture, the Israeli settler-colonial regime intentionally inflicts severe pain and causes mass suffering on the entire civilian population in an effort to subjugate and punish the community for its support of the resistance.[30] This is achieved through relentless bombing of residential areas, creating a sense of helplessness as people are unable to protect and save their loved ones, leading to feelings of shame, guilt, and a loss of control over their lives. In short, "repeated traumatic experiences under situations of totalitarian control conditions one to give up without trying, and ultimately lose all motivation and interest in life."[31] The short-term goals of these practices are threefold: first, to teach the population that resistance to Israel's control is futile; second, to support Israeli efforts in gathering intelligence on the resistance; third, to punish the population for its support of the resistance. In the long term, these extreme stress tactics are engineered to fragment society and attack the social fabric, starting with family units.[32]

Feminist scholars have shown that colonial and imperial violence are inherently sexual and must be read as such. Women's and men's vulnerabilities to sexual assault and violence must be understood as entangled within the violent colonial structure, producing the conditions of sexual assault inflicted on various populations, including women.[33]

---

29. Shehadeh, "Ghazeh El Sumud," 43.
30. Shehadeh, "Ghazeh El Sumud," 50.
31. Shehadeh, "Ghazeh El Sumud," 45.
32. Shehadeh, "Ghazeh El Sumud," 49–50.
33. Lila Abu-Lughod, "Do Muslim Women Really Need Saving? Anthropological Reflections on Cultural Relativism and Its Others," *American Anthropologist* 104, no. 3 (2002): 783–90, doi:10.1525/aa.2002.104.3.783; Rema Hammami, "Catastrophic Aid: GBV Humani-

Nadera Shalhoub-Kevorkian's work highlights the entanglements of patriarchal forces and the Israeli military colonial occupation in perpetrating sexual violence against both women and men while delineating the effects of this targeted violence on the Palestinian community. Palestinian women, since the First Intifada, have been more commonly viewed as "preservers of culture,"[34] as symbols of the nation. Thus, the women became responsible for the biological and national continuity of Palestinians. Their bodies, on the one hand, were weaponized by Palestinian patriarchy and, on the other, targeted by colonial violence.[35] Israeli sexual violence also targets men's bodies to humiliate and assert dominance, in turn depriving Palestinian men of their dignity and gendered role. Colonial and military violence interact with the internal Palestinian patriarchy, making resistance and activism complex both in private and public spheres.[36] Palestinian women, who endure life under the settler-colonial regime, face violence dually, not merely as Palestinians but also as women.[37] Indeed, Shalhoub-Kevorkian argues that

> Political conflict and war crystallize the connection between the public and the private; it stresses how the personal is political and does not disengage the "home" and the "front" as discreet or discontinuous spaces, for they are one and the same.[38]

---

tarianism in Gaza," in *The Cunning of Gender Violence*, ed. Rema Hammami, Lila Abu-Lughod, and Nadera Shalhoub-Kevorkian (Geopolitics and Feminism: Durham, NC: Duke University Press, 2023), 324–60, doi:10.2307/jj.3985462.14; Shalhoub-Kevorkian, *Militarization and Violence*.

34. Shalhoub-Kevorkian, *Militarization and Violence*, 66.
35. Shalhoub-Kevorkian, *Militarization and Violence*, 87.
36. Shalhoub-Kevorkian, *Militarization and Violence*, 79.
37. Shalhoub-Kevorkian, *Militarization and Violence*, 65.
38. Shalhoub-Kevorkian, *Militarization and Violence*, 71.

In this context, sexual harassment and rape of Palestinian women by Israeli authorities are seen as attacks on national security and the national body.[39] However, this national framing often sidelines women's pain and trauma, as internal patriarchal forces suppress cases of rape to maintain national honor. This framing marginalizes sexual violence within the Palestinian community, as injury to women's bodies lacks nationalistic significance. "Women are expected to give precedence to the homeland over their own honor" and prioritize national liberation over their own safety and well-being.[40]

In the genocide of Gazans, colonial violence targets both men and women, attacking their bodies, homes, lands, and social fabric. Since October 7, 2023, reports reveal systematic sexual violence against Palestinian detainees in Israeli military camps and prisons.[41] Palestinians — men, women, boys, and girls — are being detained in Gaza and the West Bank, where they endure inhumane and degrading treatment. This treatment includes severe beatings; withholding access to hygiene such as access to showers and bathrooms and feminine hygienic products; denial of health treatments; a starvation policy; and sleep deprivation. Various forms of sexual assault have also been reported as committed by Israeli forces, such as strip searches, with at least two Palestinian female detainees reportedly raped and others threatened with sexual violence.[42]

---

39. Shalhoub-Kevorkian, *Militarization and Violence,* 88.

40. Shalhoub-Kevorkian, *Militarization and Violence,* 13.

41. Although the crimes against men detainees such as in Sde Teiman have been particularly monstrous and reveal the sexual nature of Israeli colonialism, for the scope of this essay I will not refer to these cases. To read more, see Addameer, "Update on the Conditions and Torture Violations Committed against Gazan Detainees" (Addameer, October 7, 2024), 8, https://www.addameer.org/media/5406.

42. "Israel/oPt: UN Experts Appalled by Reported Human Rights Violations against Palestinian Women and Girls," *OHCHR,* https://

Within Gaza, according to Assiwar,[43] "this war has made the soil fertile for violence and sexual assaults, whether in places of displacement or while going to receive aid and water."[44] Various testimonies of Gazan women published during the genocide emphasize the growing vulnerability of women. Many women expressed the need for privacy during menstruation and the fear of facing gendered violence, especially after displacement by Gazan men. While sexual violence is indirectly acknowledged among women, it is rarely communicated in public. A, a thirty-six-year-old who left Gaza after the 2022 war, recounts her family's experiences amid the ongoing genocide:

> My sister refused to send her daughters to school [to take refuge] because of the amount of issues common in schools, the issue of harassment and looks, even a look [can be] harassment. Her daughters are 17 and 18 years old. She had to leave [home], and sent her daughters alone to a house where she could trust that they will not be exposed to anything, anything psychological or physical or being assaulted, and she and her husband were at the school.[45]

Women in conflict zones bear the invisible burden of caregiving, nurturing, and nursing children under extreme

---

www.ohchr.org/en/press-releases/2024/02/israelopt-un-experts-appalled-reported-human-rights-violations-against.

43. The Feminist Arab Movement in support of victims of sexual abuse.

44. Dyma Kbha, "Sexual Assault and Rape as a Weapon of War," *Faraa Maai*, June 1, 2024, https://faraamaai.org/articles/belmidan/ alaaatdaaa-algnsy-oalaghtsab-kslah-fy-alhrob. My translation.

45. Testimony 2, interview conducted on December 13, 2023, by Assiwar. All testimonies are my translation; https://assiwar.org/ campaigns/نعيش-ونحكي-شهادات-نساء-من-غزة/?fbclid=IwY2xjawGl8QpleHR uA2FlbQIxMAABHUAKGw59x1WLNT0WeUI3S9BQbfEgoCa2xJMM _2rgtL0lFC7Me1HEjda6jg_aem_QjtFOlg3zqzZD9yPVftL2Q.

conditions. Testimonies from Gaza highlight the immense responsibilities that fell upon women. They toil in the background, assuming the gendered work of preparing food, kneading dough, baking using tempered wood, caring for sick children, and keeping their families together while displaced. B., a forty-year-old woman from Gaza city, displaced by Israeli bombardment, shared the physical toll this work has taken on her. She said:

> I spend my day preparing food for my family over the wood fire that we used as an alternative to cooking gas. My chest still hurts because of the smoke I inhale every day.[46]

Similarly, a fifty-year-old refugee from Maghar, who lived in the Bureij refugee camp, explained:

> The burden is on the woman, everyone has requests for her, and it takes up space in women's lives. Look at the shape of women's faces and hands. All of our features have changed, we changed. Other than health issues, hygiene. Other than the subject of the menstruation, women are now forced to take birth control pills to prevent menstrual periods. There are no towels, this period of suffering has become more burdensome.[47]

Shalhoub-Kevorkian's research underscores women's central role in society, positioning them as resilient frontline fighters, often with limited resources.[48] Frontliners endure both the initial and final waves of violence, occupying highly visible positions of grave responsibility within daily life in

---

46. Testimony 4, delivered by the center for women in Gaza on December 19, 2023, to Assiwar.
47. Testimony 5, interview conducted on January 24, 2024, by Assiwar.
48. Shalhoub-Kevorkian, *Militarization and Violence*, 1.

conflict zones.[49] Nevertheless, women's daily practices as frontliners "disrupt, threaten, and confront power" in profound ways.[50] Despite monstrous genocidal violence, Gazan women show resilience in protecting their kin and providing better circumstances; they are "caught up in the business of creating life."[51]

Women forge new meanings to live by, resisting the totalizing forces of colonization. Shalhoub-Kevorkian shows how "keeping silent or speaking through it, emerges as a political strategy."[52] Silence, which must be listened to, speaks volumes, especially when "agency and victimization are interchangeable."[53] "Within women's victimization the conceptual parameters of agency are also clearly present."[54] Thus, power intertwined with powerlessness, along with moments of resistance, cannot be broken down into separate analytical components that simply depict a state of helplessness.[55]

However, being silent does not equate to ignorance. In Guatemala, women were silenced by a legal system that granted full impunity to perpetrators. Meanwhile, in Palestine, silence is imposed by both patriarchal national aspirations and the impunity of colonizing powers. Despite this, women's testimonies reflect a deep awareness of their insecurity.

In both Guatemala and Gaza, women work to re-member the social body, caring for families after state-sponsored disappearances or executions. In the context of genocide, as

---

49. Shalhoub-Kevorkian, *Militarization and Violence*, 5.

50. Shalhoub-Kevorkian, *Militarization and Violence*, 22.

51. Sarah Ihmoud, "Love in a Time of Genocide: A Palestinian Litany for Survival," *Journal of Palestine Studies* 52, no. 4 (October 2, 2023): 93, doi:10.1080/0377919X.2023.2289363.

52. Shalhoub-Kevorkian, *Militarization and Violence*, 126.

53. Shalhoub-Kevorkian, *Militarization and Violence*, 143.

54. Shalhoub-Kevorkian, *Militarization and Violence*, 143.

55. Shalhoub-Kevorkian, *Militarization and Violence*, 143.

Gazan women's testimonies have shown, women generally carry an extra load of invisible work that ensures the survival and well-being of their loved ones. Women's experiences offer us a gateway into the life-giving practices of the mundane. Yet while enduring violence on various fronts, women remain invisible to the Christian theological discourse in Palestine.

Divine Presence in Care

O God,
if the time of miracles has passed,
why hasn't the time of massacres?[56]

Witnessing the massacres unfold on my screen was profoundly disillusioning, as state violence stripped all sanctity from life. The sight of dismembered Palestinian bodies in Gaza and the cursed survivors compelled me to question what tortured bodies can teach us about the cross, and whether divinity can be found amid relentless violence.

The current genocide has compounded what Cedar Duaybis has called "the theological Nakba."[57] The Nakba shook many people's faith, particularly through the weaponization of the Old Testament to legitimize occupation, displacement, and, today, genocide.[58] Many Christians today have asked, "Where is God amidst genocide?" Some theologians tried to answer this question. Prominently, Munther Isaac, in a pastoral move, answered, "God is under the

---

56. Ashour, *A Gaza of Siege and Genocide*, 15, https://mizna.org/product/a-gaza-of-siege-and-genocide.

57. Cedar Duaybis, "The Three-Fold Nakba," *Cornerstone* 66 (2013): 8.

58. Naim Stifan Ateek, *A Palestinian Theology of Liberation: The Bible, Justice, and the Palestine-Israel Conflict* (Maryknoll, NY: Orbis Books, 2017), 29, https://go.exlibris.link/YP3gtVq3.

rubble."[59] But a question in return has been "Is God dead?"[60] Raheb argued that when Palestinians ask, "Where is God?" "they neither question the existence of God nor his care, but they do wonder why God is not moving."[61] Nevertheless, witnessing the extent of this genocide left many questioning God's care and presence in Gaza.

To answer these concerns, in his sermon, Isaac preached that "God suffers with the people of this land, sharing the same fate with us."[62] God's solidarity with the oppressed is incarnated in Jesus, who lived and died under Roman imperial rule. Thus, God can be found today under the rubble, suffering as he did on earth. Isaac preached that this is our consolation: God comforts us by sharing in our suffering.

In a similar vein, George Khodr, Archbishop of Byblos, Botris, and Mount Lebanon, explained that, on the cross, Jesus was not just a martyr but the unification of God with the oppressed. Jesus's humanity was perfected there,[63] where "every bleeding person bleeds with the Christ, as the blood of the Savior and the blood of the tormented are one on earth and in heaven. Every oppressed person is flogged with Christ because oppression is the same in our world."[64] The cross presents a paradox: the sovereign God endures execu-

---

59. Munther Isaac, "God Is under the Rubble in Gaza," *Sojourners*, October 30, 2023, https://sojo.net/articles/god-under-rubble-gaza.

60. This question was asked in an Arab Christian women's meeting in North America.

61. Mitri Raheb, *The Cross in Contexts: Suffering and Redemption in Palestine* (Maryknoll, NY: Orbis Books, 2017), 113. Furthermore, in his intervention at the American Academy of Religion meeting in 2024, Raheb argued that Gazans are asking, "Where is humanity?" or "Where are the Muslim countries?" instead of questioning God.

62. Isaac, "God Is under the Rubble in Gaza."

63. George Khodr, *Reflections on the Incarnation of the Word*, 2nd ed. (Beirut: Al Noor Publications, 1975), 21. All of the quotes by Khodr are my translation.

64. George Khodr, *Al-Quds*, ed. Mahmud Darwish (Beirut: Taʻāwanīyah al-Urthūdhaksīyah lil-Nashr wa-al-Tawzīʻ, 2003), 59.

tion by the sovereign regime as a consequence of Jesus's ministry of love and care. Furthermore, the cross suggests a continuation of Jesus's torture alongside the tortured others. Indeed, "the scene is one and the flagellant is another."[65]

Like Raheb, Khodr draws parallels between Jesus's life and death under Roman imperialism and the suffering of Palestinians under Zionist settler colonialism. Khodr says, "all Palestinians, regardless of their sects, have become Jesus' little brothers."[66] This unification of God with the suffering indicates an adoption, where God identifies with and cares for the oppressed. It represents a cosmic relationship that cannot be severed, regardless of the regime's brutality in destroying life and social fabric and bombs' power in dismembering bodies.

But, according to Khodr, the crucifixion is intertwined with resurrection. "Through death victory over death was completed. . . . Death was defeated by receiving the source of life."[67] Khodr proclaimed that, one day, Palestinians will rise in freedom, as Jesus rose from the dead.[68] However, history shows that Christ's resurrection did not end the evil structures of the world, nor has it stopped the greed of the military-industrial complex. The Nakba, as a "brutally sophisticated structure of oppression," has only intensified.[69]

In the story of Christ's crucifixion, state powers play the central role in weaving conspiracies, using human bodies to define who is worthy and who is to be discarded. Jesus was forcibly stripped in front of military personnel, tortured, mocked, possibly sexually abused, and crucified naked

---

65. Khodr, *Al-Quds*, 59.
66. Khodr, *Al-Quds*, 61.
67. Khodr, *Al-Quds*, 67–68.
68. Khodr, *Al-Quds*, 61.
69. Rabea Eghbariah, "Toward Nakba as a Legal Concept," *Columbia Law Review* 124, no. 4 (2024): 887.

before the crowds. State power was enacted upon his very flesh.[70] He bore the curse of the cross, a symbol of extreme violence where sovereignty claimed its power, transforming his dignified body to a brutal spectacle for crowds to witness.[71] In his final days, Jesus endured brutal state violence meant to deter resistance. The torture, whipping, public humiliation, and stripping of his body aimed to attack his honor and dignity. Jesus became a victim of sexual violence, reflecting the sexual nature of colonial violence.[72]

While the idea of God unified with the suffering can bring comfort to some, it raises theological and ethical challenges. First, despite Christian teachings on resurrection, the reality of horrific genocide makes it difficult to believe in a form of resurrection that promises material liberation. Second, how can we account for the multiple forms of violence occurring simultaneously? Indeed, we must consider the overarching structures facilitating violence. However, how can we theologically confront sexual violence, gendered violence, and other practices that Palestinian Christians typically deem wrong, when God is in full solidarity with the oppressed? Does God fully embrace these harmful practices when they are carried out by the oppressed within their community? Third, when declaring that God is on the cross or under the rubble, how can we reconcile this with the agency of those whose lives were taken, despite their own agency? Fourth, how do we reconcile God's care shown in the gospels with the genocide of Gazans? This tension challenges divine

---

70. Raheb, *The Cross in Contexts*, 48. Here, Raheb further emphasized that Jesus died at the hands of religious terrorism, in the name of God.

71. David Tombs, *The Crucifixion of Jesus: Torture, Sexual Abuse, and the Scandal of the Cross*, 1st ed. (London: Routledge, 2023), doi: 10.4324/9780429289750.

72. Tombs, *The Crucifixion of Jesus*.

presence and justice in the face of overwhelming suffering. Lastly, does God care for Palestinians only because they are victims of oppression?

I believe that the ethics of care embodied by Palestinian and Guatemalan women offers a venue for theological exploration of contradictions raised by genocide. The testimonies of Guatemalan women's work in historical remembrance and justice, alongside those of Gazan women, highlight their priority to care for their children and communities, making immense sacrifices to ensure the well-being of their kin amidst genocide. Jesus bears a profound resemblance to these women in their practices and ethics of care. Christ's ministry on earth, reflected in the Gospel accounts, calls for a new ordering of the world in which love and care take precedence.[73]

Gazan and Guatemalan women share in Christ's embodiment on earth: stripped of basic necessities, dehumanized, attacked in their most intimate spaces. Yet, they continue to reflect divine love toward their kin. Paradoxically, in times of death, women embody the truth of life and love amidst destruction.

While God can be understood to be under the rubble, united with the most oppressed, this might suggest that God has been defeated, given the absence of resurrection in our material world. Yet, the lives of Palestinian and Guatemalan women teach us about the interconnectedness of agency and victimhood. Despite facing violent realities of impoverishment, sexual colonial violence, racialization, and militarized states, women create new spaces that nurture life and safety to the best of their abilities. While theologians connect resur-

---

73. I grew up listening to many sermons on the Sermon on the Mount. The ethics of love taught by Jesus profoundly influences Palestinian Christians' daily practices, often taking precedence over other scriptural emphases.

rection to the cross, I assert that liberation is not a predetermined event following suffering. The aftermath of genocide in Guatemala has not brought total liberation or justice, and the genocide in Gaza continues. Highlighting the invisible work of care and leadership embodied by Guatemalan and Gazan women exposes glimpses of the divine in our world.

3

A New World Is Coming: She Is on Her Way

AZMERA HAMMOURI-DAVIS
Hebron and Kea'au, Hawai'i

We are hurting. Over the last year, I have found myself, like most of us, heartbroken. Enraged. Exhausted. All on repeat. As a Black Palestinian American, I am writing this at a time when both communities I identify with are suffering tremendously. Sonya Massey, a Black American woman, called the police to get help identifying whether there was a suspicious person near her home. Instead of receiving protection, she was executed. Shot three times in her face by a white police officer and left to bleed to death in her own kitchen. It was all captured on video. Among her final words were, "I rebuke you, in Jesus's name."[1] Her soul cried out for Jesus moments before she was murdered in her home. It did not have to end this way.

Meanwhile, nearly two hundred thousand Gazans are believed to have been injured or killed over the last year, with

---

1. Trevor Ault, Tesfaye Negussie, and Octavio Cadenas, "Newly Released Police Body Camera Footage Shows Sonya Massey Talking to Officers 16 Hours before Her Death," ABC News, September 5, 2024. https://abcnews.go.com/US/newly-released-police-body-camera-footage-shows-sonya/story?id=113413893.

that number increasing daily.[2] The majority of the bombs dropped on Gaza are manufactured on American soil.[3] I can still hear Hind Rajab's precious voice as she told the paramedics, "I'm so scared, please come. Come take me. Please, will you come?"[4] They wanted to come. They were on their way to rescue her. But rather than being able to provide protection, they themselves were murdered by the Israeli Occupation Forces. This utter disregard for human life cannot be the world God envisioned. Criminal legal systems that perpetuate police brutality, target, murder, and render Black and Palestinian life disposable with impunity are not new. This is the world as we have known it. And these intersecting systems of injustice are what womanist theologians like Delores Williams write against. It is what Palestinian liberation theologians Pastor Munther Isaac and Rev. Naim Ateek continue to exegete against. As we navigate this genocidal abyss, what do we do with the righteous indignation we feel in our hearts? Where are we to offer grace and mercy to our siblings in struggle as we journey toward freedom and collective liberation? I have far more questions than answers, but there are two underlying questions that I keep coming back to during this genocide: What is the substance of my faith? And what is my responsibility at this moment?

Building on the rich legacy of Black and Palestinian transnational solidarity, I am interested in what womanist theol-

---

2. Rasha Khatib, Martin McKee, and Salim Yusuf, "Counting the Dead in Gaza: Difficult but Essential," *The Lancet*, July 1, 2024.

3. Noura Erakat and Josh Paul, "Report of the Independent Task Force on National Security Memorandum-20 Regarding Israel," *Just Security*, April 24, 2024, https://www.justsecurity.org/94980/task-force-national-security-memorandum-20.

4. Emine Sinmaz, "'I'm So Scared, Please Come': Hind Rajab, Five, Found Dead in Gaza 12 Days after Cry for Help," *The Guardian*, May 21, 2024, https://www.theguardian.com/world/2024/feb/10/im-so-scared-please-come-hind-rajab-six-found-dead-in-gaza-12-days-after-cry-for-help.

ogy can teach us as Palestinian Christians enduring genocide. In this chapter, I will discuss the ways in which Palestinian liberation theology has enhanced my faith as a Black Christian woman of Palestinian descent. Then I will exegete how womanist theology can offer hope to Palestinians through the story of Hagar as she navigates the wilderness. Finally, I will reflect on how our faith has been tried by fire, and the role that both womanist and Palestinian liberation theology play in imagining freedom and collective healing.

Personal Background

As an American, I am a citizen of the empire. I have a responsibility to work to stop my government from sending the bombs that indiscriminately kill my people. As a Black woman, I inherit a history where my right to citizenship has long been denied, suppressed, and attacked by white supremacist, capitalist, imperialist patriarchy.[5] As a person of Palestinian descent, I feel the weight of generational racial trauma, having grown up in a U.S. context post-9/11 that was hostile toward Palestinians, Muslims, and Arabs. The nexus of these identities directly informs how I interpret the Bible, how I find hope, to whom I look for hope. I am concerned with understanding the ways in which certain interpretations of God limit the love God extends to those of us who happen to be farthest on the margins; God's love is never partial or conditional.

Moreover, it would be dishonest of me to act like I have always felt connected to my Palestinianness. And that was by design. I was born into a working-class, interfaith family on the Big Island of Hawai'i. My path into Christianity, or becoming a follower of Christ, was a choice I made in

---

5. bell hooks, *All about Love: New Visions* (New York: HarperCollins Publishers, 2000), 97.

high school—well before I was politicized around Palestine. Though I would later come to understand what it meant to be the granddaughter of a Nakba survivor, my journey of unlearning Christian Zionist sensibilities, as with any liberation pursuit, came as a process.[6]

I did not arrive where I am overnight. I do not believe any of us do. And I say this because, in this work of pursuing collective freedom, it is incumbent upon us to hold space for grace, change, evolution, learning, and unlearning as we fight for a better world. Grace for ourselves. Grace for the people we are in struggle with, and grace even—dare I say—for our enemies. I know that may seem like an impossible thing to imagine right now. How can I suggest we hold grace in these times when our people are under relentless persecution? While the notion of grace can be dangerous in theological discourse because it can be wielded against oppressed people to justify their subjugation, womanist theology, and especially the story of Hagar—an African slave and sex worker—helps us hold space for it all as we move toward justice.

Far too many Palestinians are tortured, ridiculed, condemned for being who they are and forced into inhumane conditions left with no other option but to find different ways to cope, to survive. I know this because it's what I have seen. Some, due to historical anti-Blackness,[7] even have been baffled when I tell them I am Palestinian. To them, my Blackness was perceived as an automatic exclusion from Palestine.

---

6. Azmera Hammouri-Davis, "A Journey of Unlearning: Reflections on Christian Zionism," *Here4TheKids* (blog), April 11, 2024, https://here4thekids.substack.com/p/a-journey-of-unlearning-reflections?r=mrgvc&utm_campaign=post&utm_medium=web&triedRedirect=true.

7. Susan Abulhawa, "Confronting Anti-Black Racism in the Arab World," *Al Jazeera*, July 7, 2013, https://www.aljazeera.com/opinions/2013/7/7/confronting-anti-black-racism-in-the-arab-world.

In the West, I was not surprised that, due to my Blackness, I was not perceived as Palestinian. I was shocked, however, to learn, once I was in Palestine, that my Blackness seemed to make me an outsider; it further disqualified me from being Palestinian.

Noura Erakat cautions us against reinforcing the same tropes and systems of exclusion in our struggle for freedom in her article "The Nakba and Anti-Blackness," not because it is the pious thing to do or the politically correct thing to do, but because it is the right thing to do if we truly want to be free.[8] And while some may view Blackness and Palestinian identity as mutually exclusive, the life of Fatima Bernawi reminds us that, in reality, there is a vibrant Afro-Palestinian community in Jerusalem, Jericho, the Negeb, Gaza, and beyond who contribute to the struggle for Palestinian liberation.[9]

Maryam Abu Khaled, an Afro-Palestinian actress born in Nazareth, reiterates the need to unlearn anti-Black racism in a viral video she posted after the murder of George Floyd in 2020. Lama Jamous, a young Afro-Palestinian journalist from Gaza, displays the truth to her nearly one million followers in efforts to end the genocide. Nada Mays, an Afro-Palestinian based in the United States, actively advocates for an end to the genocide and illegal occupation of Palestine through food justice and health equity.[10] Clearly, Afro-Palestinian women are here and always have been. And

---

8. Noura Erakat, "The Nakba and Anti-Blackness," *Jadaliyya*, July 10, 2017, https://www.jadaliyya.com/Details/34556/The-Nakba-and-Anti-Blackness

9. Elom Tamaklo, "On Fatima Bernawi, Women's Struggle, and Black-Palestinian Solidarity," *Institute for Palestine Studies*, n.d, https://www.palestine-studies.org/en/node/1653780.

10. Benjamin Setiawan, "Cooking and Coping: Making Zaatar Oo Zeit with Nada Mays," *Forbes*, March 18, 2024, https://www.forbes.com/sites/benjaminsetiawan/2024/03/18/cooking-and-coping-making-zaatar-oo-zeit-with-nada-mays/.

womanist theology asks that we contend with the realities of anti-Black racism, sexism, and classism in our assumptions of who is proximate to and loved by God. Palestinian liberation theology also shows us there is another way, offering a blueprint for collective action rooted in nonviolence, plurality, and collaboration.[11]

What Does Palestinian Liberation Theology Mean to Me?

Palestinian liberation theology came into my life when I was on the verge of abandoning my faith. I was twenty-four years old, and it was my first time in Palestine. I was the only one of my three siblings and ten cousins to get the opportunity to visit my grandfather's hometown in Al Khalil (Arabic for "Hebron"). After I saw firsthand the atrocities of apartheid to which Palestinians are subjected, I questioned why God would allow such horrific injustices to happen—let alone in the land where Jesus walked and wept. I had recently returned from living in Salvador, Bahia, Brazil where I witnessed Christianity weaponized against Black communities. I felt disenchanted with the religion, to say the least. But meeting Palestinian Christians at Sabeel Ecumenical Theological Center shifted my course. They had every right to be even more disillusioned by Christianity than I was, and seeing Palestinian Christians understand their faith as an anchor of hope rather than turning away from it compelled me to dig deeper, to sharpen my questions.

Reverend Dr. Naim Ateek's book *A Palestinian Theology of Liberation: The Bible, Justice and the Palestine-Israel Conflict* helped me understand why centering the life and teachings

---

11. Nicole Patierno, "Palestinian Liberation Theology: Creative Resistance to Occupation," *Islam and Christian–Muslim Relations*, 2015, 26 (4): 443–64.

of Jesus when reading the Bible is critical.[12] And this herme-neutic represented a symbolic lamp of hope in God's ever-lasting love and enduring commitment to truth and justice. It reinforces the notion that the gospel must mean good news for *everyone*, or else it simply is not the gospel.

The work and witness of Palestinian Quaker and liberation theologian Jean Zaru sparked the flames of God's light that gradually reawakened in me.[13] I will never forget visiting Jean Zaru in Ramallah with my dear comrade and brother in struggle, Elom. Zaru welcomed us into her beautiful home, cooked us a delicious meal, and insisted we refer to her as Teita, or grandmother. The warmth of her kitchen, the sweet smell of her knafeh, and her loving spirit felt so familiar. It reminded me of being inside my auntie's home back in the States. We read her book *Occupied with Nonviolence: A Palestinian Woman Speaks,* and I was eager to converse with her about its many themes. I recalled the first time I heard her speak to a class I was part of during graduate school. Her response to the question "How do you possibly muster the energy and courage to keep fighting in the face of such a politically bleak situation?" stuck with me. She responded, "My goal is simple. I only want to create a crack. Because where there is a crack, the light can come in. And a little bit of light can drive out a lot of darkness." Those words pierced my heart with a hope I did not know I needed. They cut through the cynicism that began to simmer and have never left me since. That is what Palestinian liberation theology did for me and what it can do for the world. It offers a beacon of light in a world rife with hatred and bigotry.

---

12. Naim Stifan Ateek, *A Palestinian Theology of Liberation: The Bible, Justice, and the Palestine-Israel Conflict* (Maryknoll, NY: Orbis Books, 1989), 11.

13. Jean Zaru, Diana L. Eck, and Marla Schrader, *Occupied with Nonviolence: A Palestinian Woman Speaks* (Minneapolis: Fortress Press, 2008), 105.

By refusing to cave into cynicism and despair when it would be more than warranted to do so, Palestinians live the command that Jesus gives to be the "salt of the earth." For, what does salt do? It refreshes food. It preserves fruit. It upholds flavor. Palestinian liberation theology helped me realize that to be Palestinian is to have faith.[14] Not just in word, but in action, day in and day out. It is to have faith that you will make it home after a hard day of work, leaving Jerusalem to return to Ramallah or while passing through Qalandia checkpoint, hoping and praying that the soldier you encounter there is in a good mood. Palestinian theology strengthens our collective pursuit of healing and justice because it invites our faith into integrity with the totality of God's creation.

Black and Palestinian Christian struggles for freedom are interdependent.[15] Where womanist theology pushes Palestinian liberation theologians to contend with race and gender, Palestinian liberation theology pushes Black liberation and womanist theologians to unlearn the erasure of Palestine in their theological conceptions of the Holy Land. They are mutually co-constitutive; our profession of faith — whether Palestinian or Black, woman, man, trans, queer, or nonbinary — is incomplete without recognizing the fullness of humanity in the other.[16] As freedom fighter and Black American civil rights activist Fannie Lou Hamer states, "None of us are free until everyone is free."[17] Rather than support

14. Zaru et al., *Occupied with Nonviolence,* 105.

15. Matthew Vega, "Black and Palestinian Christians' Struggle for Freedom," *Sojourners,* June 14, 2021, https://sojo.net/articles/black-and-palestinian-christians-struggle-freedom.

16. Toni Morrison, *The Origin of Others* (Cambridge, MA: Harvard University Press, 2017), 5.

17. Fannie Lou Hamer, "Nobody's Free until Everybody's Free," in *The Speeches of Fannie Lou Hamer,* ed. Thomas P. F. Hegarty (New York: Random House, 1992), 125.

theologies of empire and domination, we can embrace theologies of compassion, truth, and justice to navigate the wilderness of genocide.

Womanist Theology Teaches
How to Navigate the Wilderness

Womanist theologians such as Monica Coleman, Delores Williams, and Rev. Rahiel Tesfamariam urge us both to "imagine freedom" and strive to "embody freedom" so that we can "transform pain into political and spiritual power" as we usher in the new world we so long for.[18] Monica Coleman reminds us that womanist theology is a response to sexism in Black theology and racism in feminist theology.[19] Indeed, conceptions of a God who makes a way out of no way for those oppressed by racism, classism, and sexism is paramount if we intend to be morally consistent. In her seminal work *Texts of Terror*, feminist theologian Phyllis Trible outlined the various ways in which the biblical narratives have not always been good news for women. In many instances, they can be read as "texts of terror."[20] And yet, Black American women and queer faith leaders have remixed what the enemy intended for evil and allowed God to use it for good. Delores Williams makes this plain in her work *Sisters in the Wilderness*. Within our unique and painful context as Palestinians, understanding God through womanist interpretations of the story of Hagar as she navigates the wilder-

---

18. Rahiel Tesfamariam, *Imagine Freedom: Transforming Pain into Political and Spiritual Power* (Oakland, CA: AK Press, 2023), 240.

19. Monica A. Coleman, *Making a Way out of No Way* (Minneapolis: 1517 Media, 2008), 6.

20. Phyllis Trible, *Texts of Terror: Literary-Feminist Readings of Biblical Narratives* (Overtures to Biblical Theology; Minneapolis: Fortress Press, 1984), 4.

ness can teach us that God has not forgotten about us, even amidst genocide.

Delores Williams helps us understand the God who sees us all, even and especially those of us who are mistreated, abandoned, and abused by society. Williams explores the significance of Hagar's story:

> Like the slave system among the ancient Hebrews (Abraham and Sarah), slavery in the United States demanded that slave women surrendered their bodies to their owners against their wills. Thus, African American slave women (like the Egyptian Hagar) were bound to a system that had no respect for their bodies, their dignities or their motherhood, except as it was put to the service of securing the wellbeing of ruling class families.[21]

By highlighting Hagar, the first character in the Bible through whom Blackness is introduced and the first person to name God explicitly, Williams offers us a window into the situation of the oppressed from whom we can learn.

> When the water in the skin was gone, she cast the child under one of the bushes. [16] Then she went and sat down opposite him a good way off, about the distance of a bowshot; for she said, "Do not let me look on the death of the child." And as she sat opposite him, she lifted her voice and wept. [17] And God heard the voice of the boy; and the angel of God called to Hagar from heaven, and said to her, "What troubles you, Hagar? Do not be afraid; for God has heard the voice of the boy where he is. [18] Come, lift the boy and hold him fast with your hand, for I will make a great nation of him." [19] Then God

---

21. Delores S. Williams, *Sisters in the Wilderness: The Challenge of Womanist God-Talk* (Maryknoll, NY: Orbis Books, 1993), 63.

opened her eyes, and she saw a well of water. She went, and filled the skin with water, and gave the boy a drink. [20] God was with the boy, and he grew up; he lived in the wilderness, and became an expert with the bow. [21] He lived in the wilderness of Paran; and his mother got a wife for him from the land of Egypt. (Genesis 21:15–21, NRSV)

In this instance, we see that Hagar was not afraid to cry out to the Lord. She navigated the wilderness with compassion and honesty. Her innate care for her son, Ishmael, led her to tears. That honesty allowed her to release any pride or ego that would have caused her to withhold her feelings and surrender her heart to God. And as a result, God responded to her cry, letting her know she was seen by showing her the water well. Hagar was directly moved to action. She did not stay stuck in her despair. Instead, she filled the skin with water and thus was able to provide the boy with life-saving nourishment.

We can learn so much from Hagar's bravery in this moment. Hagar's heart of compassion provided clarity and courage that led to direct action. And though, as Williams points out, it didn't change the horrific circumstances she was in, the agency Hagar exercised amidst this wilderness is instructive. She refused to ignore the suffering of her child, and she refused to suppress her fear. She trusted that God was big enough to hold her doubt.

Hagar knew that, if she were to cry out, indeed God would hear her call. For "she named the Lord who spoke to her: 'You are El-roi,' for she said, 'Have I really seen God and remained alive after seeing him?'" (Genesis 16:13, NRSV). Even though she needed to find space to sit down "a hundred yards away" because she couldn't bear to see her son die, she did not turn her heart away from him. Instead, she turned her heart toward God and cried out. And God heard her. And, as a result, God walked with the boy, closely by his side as he grew up in the wilderness. He had a hope and a future. He became a skillful archer and was even able to settle in the wilderness — a most unlikely place that, once feared and full of uncertainty, now became a place where the boy grew comfortable enough to call home. This womanist interpretation of the story of Hagar could not be more relevant to us Palestinians fighting to end the genocide.

We can see Hagar's forced exile into the wilderness as analogous to the attempt to force our acceptance of a barbaric genocide of our people by the West. We did not ask for this, just as Hagar did not ask to be a forced sex worker for Sarah only to then be discarded. And yet, God affirms Hagar by proclaiming that she is seen.

What does it mean to be seen? And what do we make of Hagar being the first figure in the Bible to name God explicitly? To be seen is to be known, fully — the opposite of having to hide, the opposite of being overlooked or rendered invisible. "In a world that so often deems Black people and women invisible, Hagar boldly declares her visibility in the eyes of God."[22] To be seen suggests that "the most supreme being in the universe took the time to bear witness to the resilience and resistance of a marginalized, oppressed African woman."[23] God is intimately proximate to those of us who feel abandoned. If God spoke to Hagar, as womanists interpret this story, then surely God also speaks to and sees us Palestinians. Though the empires of the Western world dispose of us like garbage, we can find hope in knowing we serve a God who sees what we are going through, a God who has not turned away, a God who is with us in our suffering, just as God was for Hagar.

---

22. Tesfamariam, *Imagine Freedom*, 238.
23. Tesfamariam, *Imagine Freedom*, 238.

This postbellum African-American symbolic sense of wilderness, with Hagar at its center, makes the female figure symbolic of the entire black community's history of brutalization during slavery; of fierce survival struggle and economic servitude after liberation; of children being cheated out of their inheritance by oppressors; of threat to the life and wellbeing of the family; of the continuing search for a positive, productive quality of life for women and men under God's care.[24]

Many of us are navigating the unknown—a wilderness that is testing our faith now more than ever before, as we see our children and families slaughtered. For those of us in the Palestinian diaspora who call the United States our permanent place of residence, we know our government aids and abets this genocide. And, as more time goes on, we fear the creeping sense of normalization rising with every day that passes as more innocent lives are taken by forced starvation, bombardments, and disease in Palestine. The erasure of our family histories become memories we fight to preserve and protect. Through a lens of womanist and Palestinian liberation theology, we can conceive of a God who truly sees all, a God who values the sanctity of all life. Just as God valued Hagar's life when the wilderness tested her faith, Palestinian faith has been put under fire during this genocide.

Our Faith Is Purified by Fire

Our faith is churning and burning under incomprehensible pressure to figure out ways to stop this calamity. Palestinians have been confronted with many questions, by our peers, our families, and even ourselves, wondering whether there is any substance to our faith during the genocide.

---

24. Williams, *Sisters in the Wilderness*, 105.

When Paul is writing to the people of Corinth, he is reminding them of how powerful they can be together. But that power does not become fully realized until it is put to the test, until it is tried by fire. And the way they know of its durability is by assessing the foundation upon which they have built our faith. Paul goes on to say that "the work of each builder will become visible, for the day will disclose it, because it will be revealed with fire, and the fire will test what sort of work each has done" (1 Cor. 3:13, NRSV). Friends, our faith has been put under the literal and figurative fire over the last seventy-five years and especially in the past year. As Paul declares to the people of Corinth, his words minister to us today. "If the work is burned up, the builder will suffer loss; the builder will be saved, but only as through fire" (1 Corinthians 3:15, NRSV). We can find hope in knowing that we have not given up.

We are still here.

Just as Black women resist, Palestinians embody sumud—steadfastness—with every breath we take, every step we make. We embrace steadfast resilience every time we name our pain as well as our joy. We affirm God's promise. Every time we speak up, no matter where in the world we may find ourselves—whether in diaspora, in the occupied 1948 territories, the 1967 borders, or Gaza—we know that we can risk our livelihood by doing so. But not speaking is not an option. And because, as Paul says to the people of Corinth, our faith has been built on a firm foundation, the substance of our hope is something that the world can neither give nor take away. Indeed, this genocide has shown us that we have been tried by fire and purified.

Even amidst the throes of the most gruesome, heinous, barbaric genocide in modern history—even with entire families wiped off the civil registry—the spirit of evil could steal neither our hope nor our joy. Though we may bend, we will not break. We remain rooted in our faith and encouraged by knowing that "hope that can be seen is no hope at all."[25] True hope lies not in things that are seen but in that which is unseen. Paul told the people of Corinth, "Do you not know that you are God's temple and that God's Spirit dwells in you?" (1 Corinthians 3:16, NRSV). Indeed, God lives in each one of us. For each of us is made in the image of God, as Lisa Sharon Harper reminds us.[26] Paul does not say each of you *individually* is the temple of God. Instead, he very specifically addresses the people together, collectively.

It is *together* on this planet that we have been placed. Together on the land where our ancestors walked and wept, we inhabit a human experience. Together, we activate the spirit of God within. And together we shall usher in the new world. We are each other's keeper, and we can look to our ancestors to understand where our strength comes from.[27]

Black American activist Ida B. Wells heeded God's call to document the public lynchings of African Americans in the United States. Even amidst the terror of white savagery, she kept her faith.[28] But she was not naïve about the circumstances. She was not afraid or ashamed to admit that fear and doubt certainly lurked nearby. She confessed that faith and doubt go hand in hand. Doubt keeps us from being too sure of ourselves, and faith keeps us from falling into despair. Thus, a willingness to dare speak of hope must be central to

---

25. Christ at the Checkpoint, "CATC2024 Day 4: A Christ-Centered Response in Times of War — Dr. Lamma Mansour," *Christ at the Checkpoint*, 2024, https://www.christatthecheckpoint.com.

26. Lisa Sharon Harper, "Four Words That Change Everything," *Across the Divide*, April 25, 2024.

27. Jeremiah A. Wright and Jini Kilgore Ross, *What Makes You So Strong? Sermons of Joy and Strength from Jeremiah A. Wright Jr.* (Valley Forge, PA: Judson Press, 1993), 151.

28. James H. Cone, *The Cross and the Lynching Tree* (Maryknoll, NY: Orbis Books, 2011), 133.

our practice of truth-telling, as South African theologian Dr. Allan Boesak challenges us.[29]

So, what do we tell Hind Rajab's mother? What do we tell the countless other mothers, fathers, sons, daughters, granddaughters who are going to sleep tonight with an irreparable hole in their heart? We tell her our God sees, knows, and loves her daughter just as much as anyone else. We keep fighting. And we bear witness. For God's heart is not numb. God's eyes are not shut. God sees her. Just as God saw Hagar, God sees *all* Palestinian and Black people. That includes women, queer, and nonbinary folk. And neither "things present, nor things to come, nor powers, nor height, nor depth, nor anything else in all creation, will be able to separate us from the love of God in Christ Jesus our Lord" (Romans 8:39, NRSV).

Conclusion

I have learned that the substance of my faith is that hope and doubt go hand in hand, just as it did for Hagar in the wilderness. To be a person of faith is to reckon with the duality of hope and doubt indefinitely. We are not hopeless or helpless, despite what Zionism, especially Christian Zionism, would like us to believe. We also are not beyond critique and areas for improvement. We are as human as the rest of the world. Just as there are as many ways to be Black as there are to be human, so it is true as Palestinians. That means we can look at ourselves in the mirror, have room to grow, and still reserve the right to have our basic humanity honored.

There is so much work to be done, and we are stronger, as Paul reminds us, together.

---

29. Allan Boesak, *Dare We Speak of Hope? Searching for a Language of Life in Faith and Politics* (Grand Rapids, MI: Wm. B. Eerdmans, 2014), 70.

Our freedom will not come from any one person or institution. The new world that is coming does not ignore or negate the pain. As Hagar showed us, it will be born of compassion and a deep witness to the truth. Hope is not mere optimism, nor is it disconnected from suffering. Hope is a transformative, liberative force, rooted in struggle.[30] Real change emerges from the inside out. It begins with unlearning any hatred — racism, sexism, homophobia, anti-Blackness, Islamophobia, xenophobia — that we have been conditioned to believe about the other. When we treat one another as human across differences, we embody Christ's love for the church — with room for error, and space for grace, but never too far from God's love and mercy. We belong to one another, and we are who we have been waiting for.[31]

---

30. Christ at the Checkpoint, "CATC2024 Day 4: A Christ-Centered Response in Times of War — Dr. Lamma Mansour," *Christ at the Checkpoint*, 2024, https://www.youtube.com/watch?v=SyufVi2mdsA.

31. Alice Walker, *We Are the Ones We Have Been Waiting For: Inner Light in a Time of Darkness* (New York: Touchstone, 2006), 28.

4

Imagination in the Valley of the Shadow of Death

A Palestinian Christian Perspective

LAMMA MANSOUR
Nazareth

We have an incurable malady: hope. Hope in liberation and independence. Hope in a normal life where we are neither heroes nor victims. Hope that our children will go safely to their schools. Hope that a pregnant woman will give birth to a living baby, at the hospital, and not a dead child in front of a military checkpoint; hope that our poets will see the beauty of the colour red in roses rather than in blood; hope that this land will take up its original name: the land of love and peace.
— Mahmoud Darwish[1]

As I write this in the final months of 2024, Palestine-Israel lies shrouded in deep shadows, a valley filled with heartbreak and despair. Violence and devastation scar the land. In Gaza, the scale of destruction is almost unimaginable.[2]

---

1. Ashwani Saith, "Mahmoud Darwish: Hope as Home in the Eye of the Storm," *ISIM Review* 15 (2005): 28–29.

2. For more information on the humanitarian crisis in the Gaza

61

Over 75 percent of school buildings have been damaged by
Israeli attacks; human-made famine has spread with children dying of malnutrition and hunger; over 90 percent of
the population has been displaced, most multiple times;
reports of Israeli soldiers torturing Palestinians in detention
centers are rife; and the death toll from the current onslaught
is estimated to have reached as high as 186,000.[3] Many of
the Israelis who were violently taken from their homes on
October 7 remain hostage in Gaza, with leaders seeming
more interested in their own political survival than the hostages' return.[4] The wait is excruciating for their loved ones.
The situation elsewhere in the land is dire as well: the illegal
Israeli occupation of the West Bank grinds on, with sweep-
ing land grabs, home demolitions, theft of natural resources,
and unpunished settler aggression.[5] Palestinians with Israeli
citizenship, such as myself, remain the target for intimida-
tion and systemic discrimination, as compassion for fellow
Palestinians is criminalized and vilified,[6] and the state paves

Strip, see the reports by the Office of the High Commissioner for
Human Rights, accessible through their website: https://www.ocha
opt.org/.

3. Rasha Khatib, Martin McKee, and Salim Yusuf, "Counting the
Dead in Gaza: Difficult but Essential," *The Lancet* 404, no. 10449 (July
20, 2024): 237–38, https://doi.org/10.1016/S0140-6736(24)01169-3.

4. Michael Hauser Tov, "'Gambling with Hostages' Lives': Senior
Israeli Negotiator Says Netanyahu Knowingly Creating Crisis in
Cease-Fire Talks," *Haaretz*, July 26, 2024, https://www.haaretz.
com/israel-news/2024-07-26/ty-article/.premium/senior-israeli-
negotiator-says-netanyahu-knowingly-creating-crisis-in-cease-fire-
talks/00000190-ef5c-dda7-a9f7-ef7f7b210000.

5. International Court of Justice, "Summary of the Advisory Opin-
ion of 19 July 2024: Legal Consequences Arising from the Policies and
Practices of Israel in the Occupied Palestinian Territory, Including East
Jerusalem," July 19, 2024, https://www.icj-cij.org/node/204176.

6. Academia for Equality, "Report for the UN Special Rappor-
teur on Freedom of Expression," July 15, 2024, https://en.academia
4equality.com/post/academy-for-equality-report-for-the-un-special-
rapporteur-on-freedom-of-expression.

the way for criminal organizations to gain control over people's lives.[7]

In such a time, the notion of imagination may seem absurd—an unattainable luxury for a people enduring systemic violence, or an exercise in escapism that risks trivializing the gravity of the present suffering. However, as this chapter will argue, it is precisely in this valley, where violence seeks to crush every spark of hope, that imagination becomes an indispensable practice that is rooted in the hope found in Christ. This chapter posits that imagination is an essential tool for survival, resistance, and laying the groundwork for collective action. In the context of Israel-Palestine, a Christ-centered imagination asks: How would the Lord's Prayer—"Your kingdom come, your will be done, on earth as it is in Heaven" (Matthew 6:10)—materialize in the land that God incarnate walked upon?

This chapter begins by situating imagination as a spiritual practice rooted in the theology of the Kingdom of God. Then, it turns to explore three dimensions of imagination that are particularly valuable for communities living under oppression.

Imagination as the Bridge between Already Here and Not Yet

As followers of Christ, we believe in God as a living, personal, just, and all-powerful God who took on human flesh and dwelt among us (John 1:14), breaking through human history, and suffering with us and for us (1 Peter 2:22; 4:1).

---

7. Deiaa Haj Yahia, "When Murder's Not Enough: Arab Crime Groups in Israel Resorting to Ever More Vicious Methods," *Haaretz*, September 11, 2024, https://www.haaretz.com/israel-news/2024-09-11/ty-article-magazine/.premium/when-murders-not-enough-arab-crime-groups-in-israel-resort-to-ever-more-vicious-methods/00000 191-dd3c-d653-a993-dffff9de0000.

Through the cross and the resurrection, God defeated death, proclaiming that evil does not have the final word, and that God's justice and mercy will prevail (John 11:25; 1 Corinthians 15:55–58). Through this, Christ inaugurated God's reign in the world — or the Kingdom of God — which will reach its completion in the future, when all things will be made new (Revelation 21:5; 2 Peter 3:13). In the meantime, God's renewing power is at work on earth partially but substantially,[8] and we are invited to participate as co-laborers living out God's liberating reign on earth and participating in the "process through which the world is transformed"[9] (1 Corinthians 3:9; Colossians 1:13–14; Luke 4:18–19; 17:20–21).

Rooted in this understanding of the Kingdom of God, imagination, for followers of Christ, becomes the bridge between God's promise of restoration and our lived realities of darkness. It connects between what is "already here" and what is "not yet," allowing us to see glimpses of the future in the present and act accordingly. This is not escapism but "faithful realism of God's vision to bring a new humanity and a new creation," with Christ as the firstborn (Romans 8:29).[10] Therefore, when we exercise our Kingdom's imagination — envisioning the Kingdom's complete arrival with power and glory in our land — we "anticipate the impossible as the ultimate drive of all that might be possible."[11]

The prophets of the Bible led their communities in imagi-

---

8. Timothy Keller, *Hope in Times of Fear: The Resurrection and the Meaning of Easter* (Hachette, UK: Hodder & Stoughton, 2021).

9. Gustavo Gutiérrez, *A Theology of Liberation: History, Politics, and Salvation* (Maryknoll, NY: Orbis Books, 1988), 12.

10. Yousef AlKhouri, "Un-Theologizing Genocide: Stories of Love and Hate That Kill" (Christ at the Checkpoint Conference 2024, Bethlehem Bible College, May 24, 2024), https://www.youtube.com/watch?v=njSqEzOPU5E.

11. James Cochrane, "To Dream the Impossible Dream: On the Contemporary Calling of the Beloved Community in Africa," *Journal of Theology for Southern Africa* 129 (December 1, 2007): 25.

nation.[12] They called out the injustices and evil of their time while casting a vision for a redeemed future. Isaiah's imagery of a world where swords are beaten into plowshares (Isaiah 2:4) or Amos's declaration of justice rolling down like waters (Amos 5:24) are acts of imagination that transcend the present to anticipate God's promised restoration. It is our responsibility too, as co-laborers in the Kingdom of God, to paint liberation's shapes and contours according to the principles of divine love.

This imagination does not merely consist of dreaming futures. It compels action in the present. To exercise a Kingdom imagination is to embody Kingdom values in our daily life: "The fact that God has ultimate control of all injustices doesn't release us from our responsibility and mission. Our mission, similar to Jesus's, involves being sent to the world to love, serve, teach, heal, save and free."[13] We must work toward the day when the valleys of despair will be transformed into landscapes of flourishing.

Building on this understanding of Kingdom imagination as a bridge, the following sections explore how those living under oppression can harness imagination to resist injustice and actively participate in God's liberative work. From a Palestinian Christian perspective, three key dimensions of imagination are highlighted: a reclamation, a disruption, and a catalyst.

Imagination as Reclamation

Imagination is not neutral; it is a contested space. For the oppressed, engaging in imagination is an act of reclamation,

---

12. Walter Brueggemann, *The Prophetic Imagination*, 40th Anniversary Edition (Minneapolis: Fortress Press, 2018).

13. Rula Khoury-Mansour, "When the Foundations Are Being Destroyed, What Can the Peacemaker Do?," *Come and See* (blog), May 28, 2021, http://www.comeandsee.com/view.php?sid=1402.

reclaiming the realm of the possible that has been deliberately constricted by systems of domination. Oppressors seek a monopoly on imagination, embedding their vision of the future into the everyday realities of the oppressed.

Across Palestinian land, Israel has sought to entrench the exclusionary future it desires into Palestinian "spaces, bodies, and everyday engagements."[14] It presents its supremacy as "natural, neutral, and permanent."[15] The apartheid wall, the expansion of settlements, the Netzarim corridor separating the North of the Gaza Strip from the South, and the forced expulsion of Palestinian families from their homes in East Jerusalem—all of these are examples of how Israel inscribes its vision of domination into the physical and social landscapes of Palestinian life. These policies dispossess and displace Palestinians, and they shape the Palestinian collective psyche, embedding a constant state of precarity and fragility that renders freedom unthinkable.[16] This has led to what has been called a "plight of imagination" among Palestinians.[17] The ongoing Nakba has constricted the imagination of an entire people; for how can one achieve the internal safety needed to imagine a different future when trapped in a never-ending cycle of trauma?

14. Mikko Joronen et al., "Palestinian Futures: Anticipation, Imagination, Embodiments. Introduction to Special Issue," *Geografiska Annaler: Series B, Human Geography* 103, no. 4 (October 2, 2021): 277–82, https://doi.org/10.1080/04353684.2021.2004196.

15. Amanda Batarseh, "Freedom to Imagine: Reflections on the First Palestine Writes Literature Festival," *Jerusalem Quarterly*, no. 87 (October 1, 2021): 152–59 (152).

16. Yara Hawari, "Radical Futures: When Palestinians Imagine," *Al-Shabaka* (blog), March 24, 2020, https://al-shabaka.org/commentaries/radical-futures-when-palestinians-imagine.

17. Khaleel Isa and Lauriane Pfeffer, "The Plight of Imagination—Imageless Palestine," *Journal of Palestinian Refugee Studies* 4–5, no. 2–1 (2015): 29–33, https://doi.org/10.12816/0014072.

How can one envision a tomorrow when surviving today is an excruciating struggle?

Zionist forces have also sought to influence the imagination of Jewish Israelis to sustain the apartheid system of control. Israeli leaders have exploited the real threat of anti-Semitism to convince Jewish Israelis that they cannot live safe lives unless Palestine remains occupied. They have cemented the narrative that Jews will always have to "live by the sword,"[18] painting Palestinians as "human animals"[19] who "glorify death."[20] Similarly, Christian Zionists have advanced an imagination of the land as one of exclusivity and endless violence—sanctioned by God.[21] They contend that the modern nation-state of Israel is a fulfillment of biblical prophecy, and frame the struggle between Israelis and Palestinians as an extension of the struggle between Isaac and Ishmael, or even Sarah and Hagar.[22] Based on this belief, they argue that aggression and

---

18. IMEMC, "Netanyahu: 'We Will Forever Live by the Sword,'" October 27, 2015, https://imemc.org/article/73591.

19. Chris McGreal, "The Language Being Used to Describe Palestinians Is Genocidal," *The Guardian*, October 16, 2023, https://www.theguardian.com/commentisfree/2023/oct/16/the-language-being-used-to-describe-palestinians-is-genocidal.

20. "Netanyahu's 2024 Address to Congress," *Haaretz*, July 25, 2024, https://www.haaretz.com/israel-news/2024-07-25/ty-article/full-text-netanyahus-2024-address-to-congress/00000190-e6c0-d469-a39d-e6d7117d0000.

21. Munther Isaac, *The Other Side of the Wall: A Palestinian Christian Narrative of Lament and Hope* (Downers Grove, IL: InterVarsity Press, 2020).

22. Jack Munayer, "The False Paradigm of Isaac and Ishmael," *Christ at the Checkpoint* (blog), March 25, 2019, https://christatthecheckpoint.bethbc.edu/blog/2019/03/25/the-false-paradigm-of-isaac-and-ishmael; Yohanna Katanacho, *The Land of Christ: A Palestinian Cry* (Eugene, OR: Wipf & Stock Publishers, 2013); Anton Deik, "Missiology after Gaza: Christian Zionism, God's Image, and the Gospel" (Christ at the Checkpoint Conference 2024, Bethlehem Bible College, May 25, 2024),https://www.youtube.com/watch?v=GTw5U6fLO5Q&t=1718s.

dispossession in the region are necessary to hasten Christ's return, with no regard for the Palestinians who bear the wounds of this supposedly divinely ordained violence.

To imagine a different future against these narratives is an act of defiance. It is a refusal to cede the realm of the possible to oppressors who seek to control it. Empowered by God's wisdom and power, those living under oppression can challenge their oppressors and transform the reality of injustice—as can be seen in the story of Jonah as interpreted by Palestinian theologian Niveen Sarras.[23] To imagine an alternative future is to assert that another way of being is not only possible but necessary. This is a form of theological resistance: affirming the promise of the Kingdom of God that stands in opposition to systems of apartheid and domination. Assert that Kingdom of God will prevail: the upside-down Kingdom of God that challenges ethnic supremacy and hatred, where the first shall be last and the last shall be first (Matthew 20:16); the lowly are lifted and the hungry are fed with good things, the mighty are cast down from their thrones and the proud are scattered in their thoughts (Luke 1:51–53); the meek inherit the earth, those who hunger and thirst for righteousness are filled, and those who mourn are comforted (Matthew 5:3–10); where there is neither Jew nor Gentile, neither slave nor free, nor is there male and female (Galatians 3:28). In exercising our Kingdom's imagination we insist that God is close to the brokenhearted and an advocate for the orphan, the widow, and the poor (Proverbs 17:15; 22:22–23; Psalm 146:7–9; Matthew 25:31–46).

This act of reclamation is deeply grounded in the lived experiences of those who endure the brunt of oppression, as Brazilian philosopher Paulo Freire writes:

---

23. Niveen Sarras, "A Palestinian Feminist Reading of the Book of Jonah," *Journal of Lutheran Ethics* 15, no. 8 (January 9, 2015), https://learn.elca.org/jle/a-palestinian-feminist-reading-of-the-book-of-jonah/.

Who are better prepared than the oppressed to understand the terrible significance of an oppressive society, who suffer the effects of oppression more than the oppressed? Who can better understand the necessity of liberation? . . . [This fight] will constitute an act of love opposing the lovelessness which lies at the heart of the oppressors' violence.[24]

This imagination does not arise from a stance of privilege or detachment but from necessity. Maya Angelou captures this as she reflects on her poem "The Caged Bird":

The caged bird sings because it must. . . . Sometimes the melody arrived at in the cage is much more fetching, much more appealing, much more profound, much more poignant than the melody arrived at by the bird who is on the loose. The caged bird sings with a fearful trill. Its song is heard on the distant hill, for the caged bird sings of freedom.[25]

The melody of freedom, sung even within captivity, is a vital form of resistance. Despite the constrictions, Palestinian imagination still emerges in initiatives such as the Palestine Land Society's annual competition, wherein Palestinian architectural students set out plans for how to reconstruct Palestinian villages that were destroyed by Israel; or in the construction of a church by Christian, Muslim, and Jewish activists in Al-Makhrour valley despite the threat of confiscation of the land by Israeli authorities.

Palestinian imagination is not confined to formal, organized projects. In Palestine, "representations of hope—as an

---

24. Paulo Freire, *Pedagogy of the Oppressed* (New York: Seabury, 1970), 19.

25. "Conversations with Oprah: Maya Angelou" (Oprah Winfrey Network, November 17, 2013), https://www.youtube.com/watch?v=CphS2AKUB1M.

affective register attenuated to the future—are woven into the very fabric of everyday parlance."[26] Palestinian imagination is present in the daily acts of resistance and beauty that define Palestinian sumud (Arabic for resilience). It is present in the men who replant olive trees after settlers uproot them, in the women who preserve cultural heritage through tatreez (embroidery), and in the children who transform crowded, damaged neighborhoods into spaces of play and creativity. Through these practices, Palestinians defy the "limits of the injustice of the present"[27] and embody an enduring commitment to freedom and dignity.

Imagination as Disruption

Second, imagination can disrupt the despair, cynicism, and fatalism that often take root in the hearts of those living under oppression. It disrupts the narrative that oppressors' dominion is unending and hope is futile. Imagination counters despair by making space for an alternative vision, where justice, peace, and flourishing are not only possible but promised. It is an affirmation of the belief that God intends to restore shalom—a "web of relationships" that overflows with goodness between God, humans, and creation.[28] It is a commitment to partner with God in embodying God's Kingdom.

The practice of lament is central to the disruption of despair. This might seem counterintuitive, but, when there is space for grief to be expressed in a Christ-centered community, despair is less likely to find fertile ground to fester. In

---

26. Shaira Vadasaria, "Temporalities of 'Return': Race, Representation, and Decolonial Imaginings of Palestinian Refugee Life" (PhD diss., York University, 2018), 33.

27. Mary C. Grey, *The Outrageous Pursuit of Hope: Prophetic Dreams for the Twenty-First Century* (New York: Crossroad Publishing Company, 2000), 14.

28. Lisa Sharon Harper, *The Very Good Gospel: How Everything Wrong Can Be Made Right* (Colorado Springs, CO: Waterbrook, 2016).

other words, despair is often silenced grief, and the hold that grief has can be broken when it is shared and acknowledged with God and in the community of the church. In lament, followers of Christ grieve the brokenness of the world and petition God to intervene (Psalm 10; Habakkuk 1:2–4). Lament is a "liturgical response to the reality of suffering,"[29] when "holy tears" are shed in "the presence of the healing God."[30]

In Palestine-Israel—where the Nakba continues and is broadcasted for the world to see, where children covered in gray dust are pulled daily from rubble, and where war criminals with blood on their hands receive standing ovations in Western parliaments—how can followers of Christ respond? The response must begin by approaching God, as the psalmist did, and asking: "how long, O Lord?" (Psalm 13:1).

Lament refuses to accept the oppressors' normalization of injustice and insists on naming it for what it is.[31] With its unflinching honesty, lament becomes the "most visceral announcement that things are not right," making space for "a new reality, theological and social, to emerge"[32] (Exodus 3:7–10). Thus, lament threatens those in power who profit from numbness. This was starkly evident during the funeral of Palestinian journalist Shireen Abu Akleh. On May 11, 2022, Shireen was shot and killed by Israeli soldiers while reporting on a military raid in the West Bank city of Jenin. Her murder sent shockwaves of grief and anger across Pal-

---

29. Soong-Chan Rah, *Prophetic Lament: A Call for Justice in Troubled Times* (Downers Grove, IL: InterVarsity Press, 2015), 21.

30. Yohanna Katanacho, "A Cry of Pain: My God, My God, Why Have You Forsaken Me?," *Come and See* (blog), March 4, 2024, https://www.comeandsee.com/ar/post/3018545.

31. Lamma Mansour, "Being Our Neighbour's Keeper by Lamenting Injustice" (Christ at the Checkpoint Conference, Bethlehem Bible College, May 29, 2022), https://youtu.be/Hdsv8GsmO2I?si=8pb2vZC G9RuuhAsu; Cole Arthur Riley, *This Here Flesh: Spirituality, Liberation, and the Stories That Make Us* (Hachette, UK: Hodder & Stoughton, 2022).

32. Brueggemann, *The Prophetic Imagination*, 11–12.

estine and around the world, further intensified by Israeli officials' denial of their involvement—claims they later had to retract.[33] Thousands of Palestinian Christians and Muslims gathered for her funeral in Jerusalem. As the procession set off from St. Joseph Hospital, accompanied by the sound of bells from all church sects bidding Shireen farewell, Israeli forces attacked the pallbearers, nearly toppling the casket.[34] The images from that day reveal the extent to which oppressors fear communal grief, and the power of people weeping and voicing their dissatisfaction with injustice.

When coupled with a petition for God's intervention, a recognition of God's power, and an understanding of God's "unreserved [identification] with those who are humiliated and abused"[35] (Matthew 25:31–46)—that is, lament—public grief serves as a formidable challenge to the seeming victory of oppressors. Thus, lament paves the way for imagining a different reality, rooting our visions for the future in the present moment. In other words, without lament—without a sacred witness to the brutality of the present moment—an alternative imagination cannot be born.

Imagination as Catalyst

Lastly, imagination can be harnessed as a catalyst for collective mobilization and a "staging ground for action."[36] This

33. Eoin McSweeney, "Israel Defense Forces Apologizes for Death of Journalist Shireen Abu Akleh," *CNN*, May 11, 2023, https://www.cnn.com/2023/05/11/middleeast/idf-apology-shireen-abu-akleh-intl/index.html.

34. Lubna Masarwa, Huthifa Fayyad, and Frank Andrews, "Violence Then Peace: Shireen Abu Akleh Laid to Rest in Jerusalem," *Middle East Eye*, May 13, 2022, https://www.middleeasteye.net/news/israeli-palestine-shireen-abu-akleh-violence-peace-laid-to-rest-jerusalem.

35. James H. Cone, *A Black Theology of Liberation* (Maryknoll, NY: Orbis Books, 1970), 17.

36. Arjun Appadurai, *Modernity at Large: Cultural Dimensions of Globalization* (Minneapolis: University of Minnesota Press, 1996), 7.

rests on the notion that what one does today is shaped by what they believe the future can be. What one cannot imagine, one "cannot live into and struggle for."[37] Indeed, "the map to a new world is in the imagination."[38] Guided by God's wisdom and liberating power, a Kingdom's imagination allows us to draw a roadmap toward wholeness, for "without new visions we don't know what to build, only what to knock down."[39]

A Kingdom imagination is one that is beautiful, and therefore powerful. In Christian theology, beauty is a fundamental characteristic of God (Psalm 27:4), drawing people to God's goodness and truth. As people who have encountered God, we are also called to live in active attentiveness to beauty and to lead lives reflecting its essence. Toni Morrison asserted that beauty is "not simply something to behold but something one does."[40] Kingdom imagination sets out a vision of dignity, where the image of God is honored in every human being—and this is a beautiful, powerful vision. This is vividly illustrated in Isaiah 58.[41] The first five verses, where God is describing to the people their sin and hypocrisy in seeking to worship God while acting unjustly toward others, evoke a sense of heaviness and ugliness. In contrast, the remaining verses offer a promise: if people repent of their sin, turn their hearts back to God, and act compassionately toward the marginalized and the oppressed—then their "light will rise in the darkness, and [their] night will become like the

---

37. Kwok Pui-lan, *Postcolonial Imagination and Feminist Theology* (Louisville, KY: Westminster John Knox Press, 2005), 30.

38. Robin D. G. Kelley, *Freedom Dreams: The Black Radical Imagination* (Boston: Beacon Press, 2002), 3.

39. Kelley, *Freedom Dreams,* xii.

40. Toni Morrison, *The Bluest Eyes* (New York: Holt, Rinehart and Winston, 1970), 41.

41. Jo Kadlecek, "The Beauty of Justice and the Justice of Beauty," *Baptist World Aid Australia* (blog), June 21, 2022, https://baptistworldaid.org.au/2022/06/22/the-beauty-of-justice-and-the-justice-of-beauty.

noonday," they will be "like a well-watered garden, like a spring whose waters never fail" (Isaiah 58:10–11). These are images of flourishing and beauty — and they are infinitely more compelling.

Engagement in an imagination of beauty can energize and spur people into action. It cultivates what Martin Luther King Jr. called a "creative maladjustment," which refuses to normalize evil and destruction. It insists on continuing to advance the Kingdom of God, working toward the day when God will raise humanity "from the bleak and desolate midnight of man's inhumanity of man, into the bright and glittering daybreak of freedom and justice."[42]

Conclusion: The Radically Humanizing Capacity of Imagination

Imagination has been given to us as a gift from God.[43] It is our duty, then, as followers of Christ, to use it wisely and intentionally to love God and to love our neighbors. Rooted in the theology of the Kingdom of God, this chapter has conceptualized imagination as being the bridge between the "already here" and the "not yet," enabling us to hold on to God's promise of restoration and join his liberative work on earth. When understood this way, imagination can help people living under oppression to reclaim the realm of the possible, to disrupt despair and fatalistic discourses through lament and hope, and to compel bold action.

Imagination, as it was put forth in this chapter, possesses a radically humanizing capacity. When we imagine and artic-

---

42. Martin Luther King Jr., "Speech at the Annual Conference of the American Psychological Association," September 1967, https://www.apa.org/topics/equity-diversity-inclusion/martin-luther-king-jr-challenge.

43. Cheryl Forbes, *Imagination: Embracing a Theology of Wonder* (Colorado Springs, CO: Multnomah Press, 1986).

ulate a future of equality, freedom, justice, and mercy, we insist on our commitment to love and to be agents of divine love in a dehumanizing world. When we can imagine the occupier being transformed into an equal neighbor, we insist that the occupation distorts the image of God not only in the occupied but also in the occupier who was not created by God to oppress other humans.[44] When we affirm a beautiful vision of liberation that is as transformative for the oppressor as it is for the oppressed, we protect against "becoming in turn oppressors of the oppressors, but rather the restorers of the humanity of both."[45]

May God guide our steps as we imagine and work towards building God's Kingdom.

---

44. "Kairos Palestine Document," 2009, https://www.kairospalestine.ps/index.php/about-kairos/kairos-palestine-document.

45. Freire, *Pedagogy of the Oppressed*, 18.

5

Reconciliation as Co-Resistance: A Redemptive Vision

DANIEL S. MUNAYER
Jerusalem and al-Lydd

Growing up in an Israeli-Jewish school in downtown West Jerusalem as a Palestinian Christian, upon reflection, already presented indicators that a genocide was around the corner. The Israeli education system was preparing my classmates to justify or ignore the destruction of Palestinian life. Israeli politicians and military spokespersons would visit the school often, lecturing on Zionism.[1] On one occasion, the principal called my parents in to discuss my "problematic attitude" in history class. My main problem was that he refused to even mention the Nakba when teaching about the 1940s. The principal explained that he was required to adhere to the government's curriculum. He also expressed that I should understand his position, as he felt uneasy teaching Zionist history with an Arab student present in his class. I recall rejecting his explanation. I was unwilling to deny

---

1. In this chapter, Zionism is defined as a settler-colonial movement seeking to ensure a permanent Jewish majority with a Jewish state, and in the process eliminating Palestinians. See Rashid Khalidi, *The Hundred Years' War on Palestine: A History of Settler Colonialism and Resistance, 1917–2017* (New York: Henry Holt and Company, 2020).

my grandparents' forced displacement and my continued oppression. By rejecting my request and failing to acknowledge my heritage, the principal was denying my humanity — an inseparable part of my identity, rooted in my family and ancestors. This was a violent event. Unfortunately, such experiences were all too common, as many teachers, classmates, guest politicians, and military recruiters repeatedly tried to dictate my identity, redefine my history and reality, and teach me how to conform as a "well-behaved" victim. When one group of people are educated to purposefully and actively deny the humanity of another people, dehumanization knocks on the door of genocide.[2]

My experience does not reflect the daily massacres that Gazans are enduring, nor the intent to destroy, in whole or in part, the people of Gaza through starvation and blocking humanitarian aid for survival.[3] However, the erasure of a people should not be confined solely to violent measures such as extermination and genocide; it also includes more subtle measures that threaten the existence of identity and culture, including expressions of non-European Jewishness deemed unacceptable to the Zionist construction of the New Jewish identity.[4] This is a conflict between Zionist settlers and the communities they are dispossessing and erasing through policies of ethnic cleansing and occupation.

In the face of unjust suffering, Palestinians lament by crying out: "Where are you, God?" "How could you allow

---

2. Patrick Wolfe, "Settler Colonialism and the Elimination of the Native," *Journal of Genocide Research* 8, no. 4 (2006): 387–409.

3. To further understand the term and the accusation against Israel, see ICJ, "Application of the Convention on the Prevention and Punishment of the Crime of Genocide in the Gaza Strip (South Africa v. Israel)," Order of 26 January 2024, I.C.J. Reports 2024, https://www.icj-cij.org/case/192.

4. Oz Almog, *The Sabra: The Creation of the New Jew* (Berkeley: University of California Press, 2000).

such destruction and death among your children?" In the context of prolonged oppression, any authentic Palestinian theological expression must center liberation for it to witness the gospel. In other words, part of the message of the gospel in the twenty-first century for Palestinians is liberation from our spiritual and physical oppression. Ignoring liberation would render theology irrelevant to Palestinians, as it would fail to address our most fundamental concern: freedom. At the same time, due to my upbringing and exposure to Israeli-Jewish society, I deeply care for my Israeli-Jewish friends and colleagues. I understand their generational and collective trauma, and I, too, wish to see Jewish life flourish in Palestine and around the world. This prompts additional reflections: What does Palestinian liberation mean for Israeli Jews? How is liberation connected to reconciliation? And how can I continue engaging ethically with my Israeli-Jewish neighbors during such times?

Among Palestinians, it has largely been argued and accepted that reconciliation, at best, should be ignored and deemed irrelevant until our full liberation. At worst, reconciliation is seen as a tool used for our colonization. In this chapter, I will argue that a native approach to reconciliation works for Palestinian liberation. This argument will be grounded in biblical texts, Palestinian indigeneity, and other decolonial thinkers. Ultimately, this approach fosters a reconciliation process that is decolonial and contributes to Palestinian liberation, grounded in the framework of co-resistance. This may not be applicable to all Palestinians but could be helpful to those who are striving for liberation and reconciliation simultaneously. This chapter aims to build off the legacy and life work of my mentor, Dr. Salim J. Munayer (my father), both intellectually for Palestinian theology and practically for those engaged in peacebuilding efforts. It reflects both the theological insights and everyday work of

Musalaha, a reconciliation organization based in Jerusalem and Bethlehem, where I am actively involved.

Theology of Reconciliation

To understand how reconciliation works for liberation and how it can be a decolonizing and indigenizing process, even amid genocide, we must unpack a theology of reconciliation. This theological reflection on reconciliation is grounded on my own livid experience, Scripture, and Jesus's teachings.

During my school years, I vividly remember my father telling me and my brothers, "The way you treat your neighbor reflects the type of God you believe in. The distinctive mark of the Christian faith is our commandment to love our enemies." I discovered at a young age that Jesus's commandment to love is not one of submission or control defined by the oppressor's terms. On the contrary, it is a love that steadfastly refuses to accept any treatment less than the boundless love that God has for Palestinians. Love of enemy should be grounded in the confidence of knowing our self-worth, as those created in God's image (Genesis 1:27). Zionists and any other supremacists distort the image of God within themselves when they oppress and fail to recognize their shared humanity with Palestinians. When Jesus declares that peacemakers will be called sons of God (Matthew 5:9), he is revealing that God's very character is peace. Peacemakers reflect God's truest nature by actively working to bring reconciliation. Good Christian theology, therefore, must extend beyond personal salvation; it must be a source of blessing even to one's enemy, embodying the transformative power of God's love and reconciliation as embodied in Christ on the cross.

In the Garden of Eden, Adam and Eve's sin ruptured their relationship with God, with each other, and with creation, leaving them in shame and fear (Genesis 3:10). Today, sin continues to manifest not only personally but also through systems and structures that perpetuate injustice. The Israeli occupation exemplifies systemic sin, fostering oppression and hostility while destroying the foundation for healthy relationships. The incarnation of Christ restores what sin has broken (1 John 3:8). Through his life, death, and resurrection, Jesus offers reconciliation for all creation, making it the core of the gospel and a nonnegotiable mandate for Christians. As ambassadors of Christ, Paul the Apostle emphasizes that God is reconciling the world through Christ, calling us to proclaim and participate in the message and ministry of reconciliation (2 Corinthians 5:11–21). This work is central to our sanctification, compelling us to reconcile with God, our neighbors, and nature, embodying the new creation and advancing the fullness of God's Kingdom. However, based on these principles of reconciliation, the question remains, how is reconciliation possible in Palestine in a time of genocide? And how can it assist liberation and avoid colonial appropriation?

In the Christian tradition, the framework of co-resistance is a reconciliation model between oppressed and oppressor. In Exodus 2, we find a powerful example of a network of women who co-resisted against an empire's genocide. Pharaoh had commanded the killing of every Hebrew newborn boy. In the case of Moses, he was placed in a papyrus basket and set afloat on the Nile, where he was found by Pharaoh's daughter. Recognizing him as one of the Hebrews' children, she defied her father's decree, practicing civil disobedience by allowing Moses to be nursed by his biological mother. Pharaoh's order to kill only boys revealed his underestimation of women and girls. In a bold act of defiance, the Egyptian princess risked her life by partnering with the oppressed Hebrews. Not only did she save Moses's life, but she also contributed financially to the Hebrew resistance movement, making her a traitor to the Egyptian establishment.

Later in the Exodus narrative, when the Hebrews are freed from Egypt, we learn that they were joined by "a mixed crowd" (Exodus 12:38). This is significant because the liberation movement was not limited to the Hebrews.[5] It was a movement led by the Hebrews but open to all those desiring to break free from the shackles of empire. Furthermore, when the Hebrews left Egypt, some Egyptians gave them jewelry, gold, and silver, demonstrating that, in co-resistance, the oppressor class has a responsibility to aid the oppressed (Exodus 12:36). Yet, at the same time, the Hebrews needed to engage with Egyptians and accept their assistance. This narrative provides us with a biblical model of reconciliation grounded in nonviolent co-resistance. The person in power recognizes the injustice and chooses to act in aiding the oppressed, even at the risk of personal harm. The involvement of both the oppressor and the oppressed in this process shows the transformative potential of a reconciliation rooted in justice and mutual solidarity.

A New Testament example of co-resistance in the context of reconciliation is Jesus bringing together Simon the Zealot and Matthew the tax collector (Matthew 10:3–4). Simon and Matthew could not come from more ideologically opposed backgrounds. In first-century Palestine, tax collectors were collaborators with the Roman Empire, stealing from their own people and directly benefiting from the occupation.[6] In contrast, the Zealots used violent methods, such as hostage taking and assassinations, to expel their Roman oppressors.[7] They were violent freedom fighters. Jesus's calling of a tax

---

5. Mark Leuchter, *The Levites and the Boundaries of Israelite Identity* (Oxford: Oxford University Press, 2017).

6. Ben Zion Rosenfeld and Haim Perlmutter, *Social Stratification of the Jewish Population of Roman Palestine in the Period of the Mishnah 70–250 CE* (Leiden: Brill, 2020), 149.

7. Alia Brahimi, "Ideology and Terrorism," in *The Oxford Handbook of Terrorism* (Oxford: Oxford University Press, 2019), 298–315 (304).

collector alongside a Zealot was therefore highly controversial. However, both Matthew and Simon witnessed the Kingdom of God manifest in word and deed. A new creation was unfolding—a new identity that is present with the poor and marginalized while simultaneously confronting both the religious establishment and the Roman Empire (Mark 12:13–17; John 18:28–38). In this biblical example of co-resistance, Matthew had to forgo his position of privilege and join the liberation and reconciliation movement of the oppressed. Simon, on the other hand, had to abandon his violent resistance methods that risked dehumanizing the Roman occupiers and potentially turning himself into a sub-oppressor. Jesus's co-resistance offers a model that holds together both the thirst for liberation and the embrace of reconciliation, ultimately leading to the redemption of humankind.

Co-resistance within a reconciliation framework is exemplified by movements around the world such as South Africa's anti-apartheid struggle and the civil rights movement in the United States, just to name a few. These movements embraced reconciliation principles and integrated them into their foundational efforts. They acknowledged the redemptive aspect of reconciliation, which allowed for inclusion of their oppressors in the struggle for liberation, leading to meaningful outcomes. Nonetheless, reconciliation initiatives are not without their shortcomings, and we must consider their effectiveness in achieving justice and restoring relationships. Reconciliation ought to have a continued critical engagement for its applicability and significance.

Decolonizing and Indigenizing Reconciliation

After briefly discussing the theology of reconciliation and looking at examples of co-resistance, the following section attempts to illuminate how the current reconciliation work is often colonial, normalizing, and oppressive in the

Palestinian-Israeli context. Subsequently, I attempt to offer an alternative approach to reconciliation, rooting it in indigeneity.

For most Palestinians, the words "reconciliation" and "peacemaking" have become dirty words. When I share with my fellow Palestinians that I work in a reconciliation organization, it often evokes skepticism and mistrust, especially among those who have participated in "peace activities" in the past. For some, the word "reconciliation" can even evoke disgust and anger, as Palestinians view reconciliation as a colonial endeavor. These feelings are legitimate and are based on the grim reality that most peace organizations are funded by Western and colonizing powers.[8] In turn, to be eligible for financial support, the applying organization must adopt the political agenda of the donor based on their foreign policy. This means that the "intervention's" activities, outputs, outcomes, project design, theory of change, and, ultimately, impact must adhere to the powers of Western governments that are currently funding and complicit in the genocide in Gaza.[9] Moreover, research conducted by Amal-Tikva in 2020 found that the peacemaking field is dominated by Israeli Jews, who further colonize that field. Out of the fifty-two organizations researched, only 18 percent were led solely by Palestinian directors.[10] Consequently, the language of the peacemaking field is largely irrelevant to Palestinians as it does not address their political, economic, and social

8. Amal-Tikva, "The State of Cross-Border Peacebuilding Efforts: Needs Assessment on Israeli and Palestinian Civil Society Organizations," *Amal-Tikva*, 2020, 5, https://b8ofhope.org/wp-content/uploads/2024/09/August-2024_State-of-Civil-Society-Peacebuilding-between-Israelis-and-Palestinians.pdf.

9. Atalia Omer, *Decolonizing Religion and Peacebuilding* (Oxford: Oxford University Press, 2023).

10. Amal-Tikva, "The State of Cross-Border Peacebuilding Efforts," 20.

realities. Furthermore, it damages the ability for liberation-committed Palestinians to explain what reconciliation is and why it is important.

While navigating a colonized peacemaking field, we must also be aware that Israel is disrupting progress as it desires to maintain the colonial dynamic. In 2023, the Israeli Civil Administration, the governing body that operates in the West Bank, introduced a new ban on Palestinians under the age of twenty-seven from participating in peace activities in Israel.[11] The colonizer's project will transform land, property, people, and even reconciliation into objects of its dominion. Israel is obsessed with conquering and dominating the reconciliation narrative. Israel's involvement in peace processes does not come from a love for freedom, but for guaranteeing their supremacy, similar to Pax Romana. Zionism and Palestinian liberation are a contradiction in terms; they cannot be reconciled. Thus, decolonizing reconciliation means redefining the political goals and desired impact with a new language outside of Zionism. Decolonizing the reconciliation process will include challenging the hegemonic power, unlearning the colonial peace language, and undoing the colonial peace models in Palestine-Israel.

As James Cone emphasizes in the Black context in the United States—principles that hold true in any context of oppression—any effort to restore relationships between two parties, where one objectively oppresses the other, requires liberation from oppression before reconciliation.[12] In a settler-colonial context characterized by persistent structural

---

11. Hagar Shezaf, "Israel Bans Young Palestinians from Entering the Country for 'Peace-building' Meetups," *Haaretz*, February 12, 2023, https://www.haaretz.com/israel-news/2023-02-12/ty-article/.premium/israel-bans-young-palestinians-from-entering-the-country-for-peace-building-meetups/00000186-31f5-dd81-a98e-fbf737330000.

12. James H. Cone, *God of the Oppressed* (Maryknoll, NY: Orbis Books, 2020).

violence between Israeli Jews and Palestinians, this dynamic undermines Palestinian dignity and agency, preventing the possibility of authentic and holistic reconciliation. Reconciliation must therefore be led by Palestinians in our context, as they are the oppressed. It is essential for us to continue exploring Palestinian sources—our land, people, traditions, and practices—that reflect the beauty of our humanity.

To begin with, an essential aspect of an indigenous Palestinian approach to reconciliation is the location where it occurs. Thus, one of the best places to reconcile is in the desert, a neutral and safe space removed from Zionist structures and social restrictions.[13] Instead of attending conferences and workshops in hotels, going into the desert exposes people to the natural elements, connecting people's reconciliation experience to the environment, and offsetting the colonial dynamic. With limited technology and running water, the common human element is highlighted as people begin to rely on one another for their basic needs.[14] The overwhelming silence in the wilderness becomes an opportunity to reconnect with the divine and the "other" and to engage in deep self-reflection, leading to decolonial possibilities.

In the Abrahamic religions, the desert has always been a sacred space where God reveals Themselves to humanity. Interestingly, the Hebrew word for desert, midbar (מדבר), shares its root with the word for speech, daber/dvar (דבר), emphasizing the desert as a place where God speaks. Yet, encountering God in the desert often brings profound challenges. As illustrated by Moses's transformative time among the Arab Midianites, he let go of his imperial identity and embraced his purpose to liberate his people from oppression

---

13. Salim J. Munayer, *Journey through the Storm: Lessons from Musalaha Ministry of Reconciliation* (London: Langham Creative Projects, 2020).

14. Musalaha, "Musalaha: A Curriculum of Reconciliation, Chapter 2—Stages of Reconciliation," *Musalaha*, 2020 (link unavailable).

(Exodus 2:11–21). Elijah, fleeing from Jezebel, found himself in the desert under a tree, where God revealed Themselves and encouraged him to continue his prophetic mission (1 Kings 19:1–15). John the Baptist began his ministry in the desert, urging men and women to repent, and prepare for the coming of the Lord (Matthew 3:1–6). After his baptism, the Spirit led Jesus into the desert, where he spent forty days being tempted by Satan (Matthew 4:1–11). Also, in the Islamic tradition, it is believed that the Quran was revealed to the Prophet Muhammad on Jabal al-Nour in the desert (Quran 96:1–5). Undoubtedly, the silence and stillness of the mystical desert provide a unique space for encountering God and a setting for individuals to confront life's challenges and embrace a renewed mission.

A second decolonial source is Sulha. Sulha is a traditional Arab method of peacemaking rooted in communal values of collective responsibility.[15] Palestinians use sulha to solve conflicts at an intracommunity level. The process of sulha is intergenerational, with elders playing a central role in offering wisdom and guidance.[16] Sulha often combines mediation and arbitration with relevant considerations of honor-based communities.[17] In addition, hospitality, food, and sharing gifts further demonstrate the sincerity of repentance and the commitment to repairing relationships. That is to say, Israeli Jews must realize that indigenizing reconciliation is a costly experience. It is much more than appreciating our delicious falafel, rhythmic dabke, and glamorous tatreez; it means deconstructing their Zionist identity and narrative. If Israeli

---

15. Jean Zaru, "Occupied with Nonviolence," in *Christian Theology in the Palestinian Context*, ed. Rafiq Khoury and Rainer Zimmer-Winkel (Berlin: AphorismA, 2019).

16. Samer Fares, Feras Milhem, and Dima Khalidi, "The Sulha System in Palestine: Between Justice and Social Order," *Practicing Anthropology* 28, no. 1 (2006): 21–27.

17. Fares et al., "The Sulha System."

Jews were to engage in sulha, it would require reparations, multigenerational repentance, and public acknowledgment of colonial violence. Joining processes such as sulha will require vulnerability and surrendering privilege. Only those prepared to join the indigenous processes will experience true fellowship with Palestinians and reconciliation. At the same time, for this to happen, Palestinians must be willing to share and teach their indigenous ways of community, forgiveness, and peacemaking.

While sulha offers a powerful alternative to Zionist state-driven systems, it is not without its limitations. The process can often be patriarchal, restricting the participation of women. Despite this obstacle, sulha can be a dynamic method to build on, offering a framework rooted in Palestinian indigeneity.

Reconciliation Works for Liberation

At times of occupation and genocide, it is possible to view reconciliation and liberation as complete opposites. Nevertheless, I am going to demonstrate how reconciliation can work for liberation and vice versa. They are interdependent.

A reconciliation that works for liberation cannot be neutral toward the sins of injustice. It begins with resisting oppressive powers and rejecting the notion that some humans are superior to others because they are "chosen." Reconciliation holds Israeli Jews accountable to the cause of Palestinian liberation.[18] In our context, who can better grasp the suffering of the crucified Christ? Zionists who oppress and kill through their use of power cannot draw from that same power the strength to liberate either Palestinians or themselves. We cannot expect Israeli Jews and Westerners to lead

---

18. Taken from Cone, *God of the Oppressed*, 238, and applied to the Palestinian context.

the reconciliation process in Palestine-Israel, because their worldview is defined by privilege benefiting from an unjust system. Expecting the Israeli Jews to lead the liberating reconciliation process in Palestine-Israel is the equivalent of expecting white Americans to lead the civil rights movement in the United States or white South Africans to lead the anti-apartheid movement in South Africa. How can Israeli Jews articulate what oppressed Palestinians need without living in our shoes? The vocation of liberation is always given to all of humanity, but it ought to be led by the oppressed to restore harmonious relationships.[19]

Yet, there are those in the Palestinian liberation camp who deny or fail to grasp the need for reconciliation within the liberation movement. In our struggle for liberation from Zionist colonialism, we must remain vigilant against the existing dangers of becoming sub-oppressors ourselves.[20] Decades of living under settler-colonial violence shapes Palestinians, leaving our liberation struggle vulnerable to adopting the oppressors' structures and conditions.[21] I often hear Palestinians claim that our liberation means merely ending the occupation. While ending Israeli military occupation is essential, it does not provide an alternative model of humanity. A vision of liberation without reconciliation risks becoming a role reversal, in which the oppressed adopt the oppressor's structures and practices to become the new rulers of the land and people.

All liberation struggles must confront this phenomenon. Consider the Palestinian Authority (PA), born out of the liberation movement, which transformed into an entity that privatized liberation for Palestine's elite.[22] It adopted Israel's

19. Paulo Freire, *Pedagogy of the Oppressed: 50th Anniversary Edition* (London: Bloomsbury Publishing, 2018).

20. Freire, *Pedagogy of the Oppressed*.

21. Freire, *Pedagogy of the Oppressed*.

22. Megan Giovannetti, "Palestinians Furious and Fed Up with

oppressive structures through collaboration with Israel to suppress Palestinians and dismantle liberation initiatives. Hamas, similarly to the PA, is a sub-oppressor when it adopts an exclusively Islamic vision and participates in unjust acts of violence.[23] Hamas's liberation project may substitute Jewish supremacy with Islamic supremacy, which risks oppressing non-Muslim inhabitants and other Muslims. When the oppressed become the oppressors, the model of humanity remains unchanged, only wearing different masks.[24] However, it is crucial to emphasize that, while the PA and Hamas obstruct and complicate liberation from the Zionist project, they cannot be equated with those who created and sustain the oppression. Indeed, liberation and reconciliation are two different sides of the same coin; one without the other leads to further oppression.

Drawing back on the theology of reconciliation, we see that Paul understood the importance of the new model of humanity and the cycle of oppressor and oppressed. In his letter to the Galatians, Paul writes, "So in Christ Jesus you are all children of God through faith, for all of you who were baptized into Christ have clothed yourselves with Christ. There is neither Jew nor Gentile, neither slave nor free, nor is there male and female, for you are all one in Christ Jesus." Paul was not advocating for "race-class-gender blindness" but highlighting the liberating and reconciling model offered by Jesus. This model emphasizes that the oppressed must not reclaim their humanity by becoming sub-oppressors, whether knowingly or unknowingly. Instead, they should

---

Corruption of Abbas's 'Mafia' PA, *Middle East Eye*, 2019, https://www.middleeasteye.net/news/palestinians-furious-and-fed-corruption-abbass-mafia-pa.

23. MEE Staff, "Hamas in 2017: The Document in Full," *Middle East Eye*, 2017, https://www.middleeasteye.net/news/hamas-2017-document-full.

24. Freire, *Pedagogy of the Oppressed*.

aim to dismantle all forms of oppression, restoring humanity to both the oppressor and the oppressed. To put it differently, the Palestinian struggle for liberation and our commitment to humanity are inseparable from how we engage with our Zionist adversaries. Palestinians must recognize that, when we embrace the struggle for liberation, we take on the full responsibility of that struggle. This responsibility involves envisioning and committing ourselves to building a new model of humanity that transcends the native-settler dichotomy, creating a new human identity as we move toward freedom from oppression.[25] Those who refuse to direct liberation toward reconciliation risk preserving the current violent model of humanity and, potentially, turning liberation itself into an idol.

Methods and Implications of Co-Resistance

In this section, I want to address the elephant in the room: how can we Palestinians ethically engage in a reconciliation process with our Israeli Jewish neighbors in times of genocide? This is undoubtedly one of the most difficult and sensitive questions with which I wrestle. To clarify, I am not suggesting that all Palestinians must engage with Israeli Jews in their individual struggle for liberation, especially not Gazans. However, I suggest that the Palestinian cause could benefit from further clarity in articulating how we might practically engage with Israeli Jews or communicate how we would like them to engage with us, if at all. Love of neighbor and enemy requires more than avoidance or mere advocacy. Speeches, lectures, conferences, and statements alone are insufficient in the face of genocide; when commanded

---

25. Mahmood Mamdani, *Neither Settler Nor Native: The Making and Unmaking of Permanent Minorities* (Cambridge, MA: Harvard University Press, 2020).

to love, the oppressed need tangible action to ground intellectual discourse. Only when intellect and action unite can true change occur.

The violence of Zionism is passed down from generation to generation, making Israeli Jews heirs to supremacist identities. Yet, in my reconciliation work, I encounter a significant number of Israeli Jews who are rejecting some or all of the values of the Zionist project that preaches democracy while imposing apartheid. Thus, for Palestinians who understand the importance of engaging Israeli Jews, I am going to categorically provide guidelines for engaging with three different types of Israeli Jews: Israeli Jews who are unwilling to listen and recognize the humanity of Palestinians (group 1); Israeli Jews who are willing to listen and engage with Palestinians in dialogue (group 2); and post-Zionist Israeli Jews who are willing to take action and join the Palestinian liberation and reconciliation movement (group 3). To clarify, I am not suggesting that these identities are static. Rather, I am referring to a spectrum of Zionism upon which Israeli Jews fluctuate but still maintain an underlying baseline within that spectrum.

The first group of Israeli Jews consists of individuals who refuse to recognize the humanity of Palestinians. They are fully aware that our liberation would not align with their Zionist interests, and they actively sabotage our struggle for humanization. They seek to keep Palestinians oppressed or have us entirely erased. The majority of group 1 will never participate in a reconciliation process, but, for those who occasionally do, they often show up as spokespersons for the Israeli government, justifying its sins and spreading disinformation. Given the context and circumstances, each Palestinian must decide whether engaging is worth their time and the toll it will take on their being as they are forced to justify their humanity. If one chooses to engage, love in this violent context means challenging and confronting the lies and myths of the settler-colonial narrative and identity. Whether motivated by the humanity of Zionists or the attention of listening bystanders, one should never accept dehumanization. The oppressed must reclaim their dignity and, in the confrontation, leave the Zionists challenged. After the confrontation, Palestinians must assess the potential dangers, as some may seek to harm you, while others might actively persecute you.

The second group of Israeli Jews are persons who have partially or fully discovered themselves as oppressors. Their realizations may cause them considerable anguish, but it has not led them to true solidarity with Palestinians. These Israeli Jews rationalize their guilt with fear and zero-sum-game scenarios, all while clinging to their privilege. They have yet to risk the act of love. Real solidarity requires immersing oneself in the reality of Palestinians and fighting alongside us to transform the oppressive conditions under which we live. Essentially, this group of Israeli Jews begins to consider themselves oppressed as they start sacrificing their privilege.[26] Embracing equality feels restrictive and threatening as they begin to remove their "birthright." These are Israeli Jews who engage in reconciliation activities with good intentions, but the settler-colonial identity still has a grip on them. They believe in equality and human rights for all but also desire security through supremacy within a Jewish state and serve in the Israeli military at the expense of Palestinian lives.

Their semicritical reflections have not yet been translated into action for the oppressed. They may protest for a ceasefire or the return of Israeli-Jewish hostages but fail to address the root causes of the settler-colonial conflict. Each

---

26. Taken from Freire, *Pedagogy of the Oppressed*, 57, and applied to the Palestinian context.

Palestinian must evaluate every situation and individual on a case-by-case basis. If one chooses to engage, the engagement should be rooted in love, expressed through education, dialogue, and, when necessary, confrontation. I am not suggesting that Palestinians normalize injustice by prioritizing friendship over ethics. On the contrary, we must share our full truth and position regarding our struggle for liberation. Most group-2 Israeli Jews participating in reconciliation activities are open to listening and reflecting. However, their capacity to unlearn Zionism and redefine their identity in ways that inspire action will depend on a range of personal and contextual factors.

The third group, post-Zionist Israeli Jews, consists of individuals who have rejected settler colonialism and embraced a new value system defined by the Palestinian struggle for liberation. These Israeli Jews have died to Zionism and are reborn to co-resist with Palestinians against Zionist oppression. This is a form of decolonial baptism, often a painful and transformative process. I argue that reconciliation requires the Palestinian liberation movement to make room for these Israeli Jews, who are often considered traitors within their own communities. Rejecting them at this point would have more to do with "who they are" as opposed to "what they do," which risks portraying the liberation movement as racist and exclusive. Moreover, it provides ammunition to the Zionist camp, which seeks to pull these post-Zionist Israeli Jews back into the settler-colonial fold.

These Israeli Jews join reconciliation activities because they are ready and willing to take action.[27] They are ready to love and pay the price for it. Nonetheless, Israeli Jews joining the Palestinian liberation movement require clear parameters, and there are two main risks to highlight in these situations. First, once Israeli Jews cease to be active or inactive oppres-

---

27. Taken from Freire, *Pedagogy of the Oppressed*, 49.

sors and join the Palestinian struggle, they may assume leadership in the reconciliation process.[28] Despite their good intentions and desire to transform oppression, many may lack confidence in Palestinians' ability to think, organize, and lead our own liberation movement. Israeli Jews committed to the Palestinian cause must consistently self-reflect and examine their roles. We must be cautious of those who wish to dominate the reconciliation process and do not trust Palestinian capabilities. A true co-resistor can be identified by their ability to trust and be led by Palestinians and, through that trust, form comradeship with the oppressed.[29] Second, it must be made clear that it is for Palestinians to decide the authenticity of Israeli-Jewish conversion and their place in the Palestinian struggle for liberation.[30] Accountability is essential for Israeli Jews who share our struggle. When co-resisting the powers of evil, it is the role of Palestinians to make space for post-Zionist Israeli Jews in our movement, but it is also our responsibility to define their place.

Conclusion: Reconciliation Is Redemption

Reconciliation is a difficult and painful task, especially during times of occupation and genocide, yet it remains an essential Christian mandate for spirituality and discipleship. This chapter has sought to demonstrate that reconciliation encapsulates the essence of Jesus's teachings through a framework of co-resistance, offering a redemptive way forward for oppressors, sub-oppressors, and the oppressed. It is a commitment to joining God's work of bringing justice by transforming the political, economic, and social structures that dehumanize people. Additionally, this chapter

---

28. Taken from Freire, *Pedagogy of the Oppressed*, 60.

29. Taken from Freire, *Pedagogy of the Oppressed*, 60.

30. Taken from Cone, *God of the Oppressed*, 242, and applied to the Palestinian context.

has explored how a decolonial Palestinian approach to reconciliation introduces a new model of creation, where the one who liberates also reconciles, and the one who reconciles also liberates. This creates a possibility for redemption that dissolves the distinction between oppressed and oppressors among Palestinians and Israeli Jews. It envisions a reconciled reality that provides freedom for Palestinians while inviting Israeli Jews to become more indigenous—a subject that warrants further exploration in another setting.

It is also important to note the limitations of this chapter, as it offers a Christian-centric articulation of reconciliation that may be less applicable to individuals from other or no faith traditions. Nonetheless, I hope my contribution adds intellectual depth to the ongoing conversation within Palestinian theology and offers practical guidance for peacebuilding practitioners. Several areas remain to be further developed, such as a theology of co-resistance, a deeper diagnosis of the colonial peacebuilding field in Palestine-Israel, exploration of more indigenous Palestinian reconciliation practices, and additional practical guidelines for reconciliation. Looking ahead, I see reconciliation as a redemptive process of breaking down the dividing wall of hostility (Ephesians 2:14), and restoring relationships to their original state in the Garden of Eden—equalizing Palestinians and Israeli Jews and maintaining that balance. This reality includes a new family of God that meets everyone's needs, living in the hope of a new Jerusalem and a new creation (Revelation 21:1–4). In the meantime, as apartheid continues, it calls for a willingness to lay down one's life by partaking in God's liberating and reconciling work, anticipating the day when heaven and earth are fully realized, and genocide is no longer a word in the vocabulary of humankind.

6

Noticing Sumac in Unexpected Places

Engaging Palestinian and North American Indigenous Writings on Land

SHADIA QUBTI
Nazareth

During the initial phase of my studies in Vancouver, the process of acclimatization to a new environment involved curious exploration of the local flora and landscapes. A striking realization during my explorations was the presence of the sumac tree (*Rhus spp.*), a species native to both Palestine and North America. In Palestine, sumac is predominantly found in the mountainous regions in the West Bank and upper Jordan Valley and serves as a key ingredient in traditional Palestinian cuisine, namely, Palestinian Mosakhan, and in medicinal practices.[1] Similarly, in North America, the smooth sumac (*Rhus glabra*) is native to the region referred to as Turtle Island by many Indigenous peoples, where it holds significance in both culinary and medicinal practices.[2] The ubiquity of sumac across Canadian landscapes serves as a

---

1. "Sumac — Plants of Palestine," Mahmiyat, https://www.mahmiyat.ps/en/flora-and-fauna/330.html.

2. Scott Kloos, *Pacific Northwest Medicinal Plants: Identify, Harvest, and Use 120 Wild Herbs for Health and Wellness* (Portland, OR: Timber Press, 2017), 306.

metaphorical representation of my growing awareness of Indigenous presence and struggles in North America. This botanical parallel facilitated a process of critical examination and deconstruction of preconceived notions about Canadian society, ultimately leading to a more nuanced understanding of the interconnected historical and contemporary experiences of Palestinian and North American Indigenous peoples.

The Current Context: Gaza's Ongoing Nakba and Global Indigenous Solidarity

As of this writing (August 2024), Gaza has been enduring a nine-month (continued) Nakba, resulting in over 39,000 Palestinian fatalities, with an additional 10,000 individuals presumed buried under the rubble.[3] About 2.3 million Palestinians have been displaced, some multiple times, while health care, education, housing, and agriculture have been devastated, rendering Gaza nearly uninhabitable. Amid this genocide, a global movement has become more visible, calling for an end to this genocide and supporting the pursuit of justice for Palestinians.

The solidarity between Indigenous peoples and Palestinians has manifested in diverse and powerful ways. This alliance extends beyond mere symbolic gestures, encompassing cultural exchanges, artistic expressions, and joint activism. Indigenous women have incorporated Kufiyehs, the traditional Palestinian scarf, into their regalia during protests, symbolically weaving together their struggles.[4]

---

3. "Explainer: Gaza Death Toll: How Many Palestinians Has Israel's Campaign Killed?" Reuters, July 26, 2024, https://www.reuters.com/world/middle-east/gaza-death-toll-how-many-palestinians-has-israels-campaign-killed-2024-07-25/.

4. Richie Assaly, "Why Some Indigenous Advocates and Palestinians Feel They're 'Natural Allies,'" *Toronto Star*, May 6, 2024, https://

Reciprocally, Palestinians in Gaza have performed Native American dances, demonstrating a shared spirit of resistance.[5] Indigenous artists across North America have created works explicitly supporting the Palestinian cause, ranging from visual art to music and poetry.[6] These expressions of solidarity are not isolated incidents but part of a growing movement that recognizes the parallels between their experiences of colonization and dispossession. Organizations like Indigenous Solidarity with Palestine have emerged, facilitating ongoing dialogue and collaborative actions.[7] This multifaceted solidarity reflects a deep recognition of shared histories and a commitment to mutual support in the face of ongoing colonial practices. This chapter explores two key questions from my perspective as a Palestinian theologian: "What insights can I gain from

www.thestar.com/news/canada/why-some-indigenous-advocates-and-palestinians-feel-they-re-natural-allies/article_685ba94d-336e-512e-8126-06d40abd509e.html.

5. btReport, "A Palestinian Danced the Dabke during the Clashes 'Freedom Dance' 'Death Dance,'" YouTube, November 17, 2023, https://www.youtube.com/watch?v=7CjJ9L75_Gk&t=43s.

6. Molly Lipson, "The Indigenous Artists Creating Work in Solidarity with Palestine," Hyperallergic, May 24, 2024, https://hyperallergic.com/917454/indigenous-artists-victor-pascual-nipinet-landsem-dani-elle-seewalker-creating-work-in-solidarity-with-pales tine/; Phil Grey (Tsimshian and Mikisew Cree), "Battikh," Cedar Roots Collective, 2024, https://cedarrootscollective.ca/collections/battikh; Ian Reid (Heiltsuk and Tsimshian), "We Stand with Palestine," Cedar Roots Collective, 2024, https://cedarrootscollective.ca/collections/we-stand-with-palestine-by-nusi-ian-reid; "Indigenous Solidarity Letter with Palestine," The Red Nation, October 27, 2023, https://thered nation.org/statement-of-indigenous-solidarity-with-palestine.

7. This network advocates for decolonization as the only path to justice, calls for solidarity between Native American and Palestinian liberation movements, and emphasizes the connections between historical US policies toward Indigenous peoples and current US support for Israel. See Indigenous Solidarity with Palestine, https://indige nousforpalestine.org.

North American Indigenous theologians who have been experiencing settler colonialism and genocide long before my people?"[8] and "How might their theological perspectives inform my understanding of the ongoing situation in Palestine?"[9]

This chapter explores these connections through several lenses: examining current Indigenous–Palestinian solidarity movements, analyzing shared experiences of settler colonialism, and investigating the parallel weaponization of biblical texts against both communities. Through this analysis, I pro-

---

8. Unlike traditional colonialism, which primarily seeks to extract resources and labor from Indigenous populations while maintaining colonial rule from abroad, settler colonialism aims to permanently occupy Indigenous lands and replace Indigenous populations with a new settler society. Settler-colonial projects, as seen in North America and Palestine/Israel, are characterized by the ongoing displacement of Indigenous peoples, appropriation of land (rather than just resources), and establishment of new political/legal structures that normalize settler sovereignty while erasing Indigenous presence and claims to the land. See Patrick Wolfe, "Settler Colonialism and the Elimination of the Native," *Journal of Genocide Research* 8, no. 4 (December 2006): 387–409, https://doi.org/10.1080/14623520601056240; Lorenzo Veracini, *Settler Colonialism: A Theoretical Overview* (Basingstoke: Palgrave Macmillan, 2010).

9. Regarding theology, it is important to note that this term and its academic framework are rooted in Western thought. Some Indigenous scholars, such as Tink Tinker (Osage) and Richard Twiss (Cree), have pointed out that theology is not a natural category of analysis for Indigenous peoples, but rather a European category imposed on them. When discussing Indigenous spiritual perspectives, I attempt to use terminology and frameworks that respect Indigenous ways of knowing and being, while acknowledging the limitations of applying Western theological concepts to Indigenous spiritualities. See George (Tink) Tinker, "Native American Theology," in *Liberation Theologies in the United States: An Introduction*, ed. Stacey M. Floyd-Thomas and Anthony B. Pinn (New York: New York University Press, 2010), 168–80 (171); Richard Twiss, *Rescuing the Gospel from the Cowboys* (Downers Grove, IL: InterVarsity Press, 2015), 59; Margaret Kovach, *Indigenous Methodologies: Characteristics, Conversations, and Contexts* (Toronto: University of Toronto Press, 2009), 12.

pose new frameworks for Palestinian-Indigenous theological dialogue that move beyond critique to create spaces for mutual learning and reimagining relationships with land.

Theorizing Settler Colonialism:
A Palestinian-Indigenous Framework

Mike Krebs (Blackfoot) and Dana Olwan trace Palestinian-Indigenous solidarity to the 1970s in Canada, noting its evolution into a transnational movement. These solidarities are apparent in both academic and activist spheres and inform each other. They bring concrete examples of the shared experiences of colonization in Palestinian and North American Indigenous contexts. The authors identify three main similarities between Canadian and Israeli settler-colonial practices: land displacement and resource theft, control of Indigenous movement, and the use of negotiations to entrench occupation.[10] A striking example of these parallels is seen in the control of Indigenous movement. In Canada, this was exemplified by the Pass System, which restricted the movement of Indigenous people off reserves. Similarly, in the occupied Palestinian territories, an extensive system of permits, checkpoints, and the apartheid wall regulates and restricts Palestinian movement. The siege of Gaza since 2006 further illustrates this control. In both contexts, these systems of movement control serve to maintain settler dominance and limit Indigenous access to land and resources. This parallel demonstrates how settler-colonial projects, despite geographical and historical differences, employ similar tactics to exert control over Indigenous populations and territories. However, Krebs and Olwan caution against oversimplify-

---

10. Mike Krebs and Dana M. Olwan, "'From Jerusalem to the Grand River, Our Struggles Are One': Challenging Canadian and Israeli Settler Colonialism," *Settler Colonial Studies* 2, no. 2 (2012): 144–51, https://doi.org/10.1080/2201473x.2012.10648846.

ing these comparisons, acknowledging the unique aspects of each context while highlighting these shared characteristics of settler colonialism.

Waziyatawin, a Dakota scholar, identifies significant differences between settler-colonial practices in the United States and the modern State of Israel, particularly in how Indigenous peoples are perceived and treated. A striking example of this difference is the concept of "imperialist nostalgia" present in the American context but absent in Israel.[11] In the United States, settlers often display a desire to recognize the historical presence of Indigenous peoples without relinquishing power or control. This is exemplified by left-leaning settlers' efforts to reinstate Indigenous place names while maintaining ownership and control over these sites. This practice allows settlers to acknowledge Indigenous history superficially while avoiding meaningful repatriation or power-sharing. In contrast, Israeli settlers do not engage in such nostalgic practices, as they view Palestinians as an ongoing threat rather than a subjugated population. Instead, as Mitri Raheb points out, there's a systematic renaming of Palestinian places with biblical Hebrew names, aiming to erase Palestinian history and presence rather than acknowledge it.[12] This difference highlights how the stage and perception of Indigenous resistance shape settler-colonial attitudes and practices in these two contexts.

Furthermore, their findings inform their solidarity primar-

---

11. Waziyatawin, "Malice Enough in Their Hearts and Courage Enough in Ours: Reflections on US Indigenous and Palestinian Experiences under Occupation," *Settler Colonial Studies* 2, no. 1 (2012): 172–89 (181).

12. Specifically, Raheb discusses this topic in a section called "The Power of Naming Things"; see Mitri Raheb, "The Bible and Land Colonization," in *Theologies of Land: Contested Land, Spatial Justice, and Identity*, ed. Khiok-Khng Yeo and Gene L. Green (Eugene, OR: Cascade Books, 2021), 8–37 (23–25).

ily in North America. These conversations are informative and valuable, in that they highlight the social and political impacts on Indigenous peoples and their co-resistance efforts. Co-solidarity revolves around various forms of mutual support and co-resistance to settler colonization between Palestinians and North American Indigenous peoples. Scholars such as Krebs and Olwan, and Chandni Desai, explore ways to foster global solidarity while addressing specific struggles for sovereignty and self-determination in both contexts.[13] They emphasize the importance of recognizing the unique aspects of each settler-colonial situation, including gendered and racialized dimensions, while also identifying shared experiences of oppression. This co-solidarity is manifested through academic engagement, as seen in the North American Indigenous Studies Association's (NAISA) endorsement of the academic Boycott, Divestment, and Sanctions (BDS) movement and through on-the-ground activism and mutual support during protests and land reclamation efforts.[14] The concept of "Inter/National" solidarity, developed by Steven Salaita, further emphasizes the transnational nature of these

13. Chandni Desai, "Disrupting Settler-Colonial Capitalism: Indigenous Intifadas and Resurgent Solidarity from Turtle Island to Palestine," *Journal of Palestine Studies* 50, no. 2 (2021): 43–66 (44).

14. NAISA's statement on Palestine condemns "in the strongest possible terms the Israeli genocide in Gaza and the ongoing settler colonial elimination targeting Palestinians," and calls for "an immediate ceasefire, immediate access for humanitarian aid, an impartial investigation into all atrocities committed, an end to the illegal occupation of Palestinian lands, and the right of return for Palestinian refugees." NAISA reaffirms its 2013 commitment to the academic boycott of Israeli institutions, stating, "We issue this current statement in the spirit of our 2013 statement" that strongly protested "the illegal occupation of Palestinian lands and the legal structures of the Israeli state that systematically discriminate against Palestinians and other Indigenous peoples"; see "NAISA Council Statement on Palestine," Native American and Indigenous Studies Association, May 7, 2024, https://naisa.org/about/council-statements/naisa-council-statement-on-palestine.

connections. However, as Waziyatawin notes, this solidarity also involves recognizing differences in resistance strategies and aspirations, highlighting the complexity of these relationships beyond simple parallels of shared suffering.

Waziyatawin offers a different view of co-solidarity based on her visit to occupied Palestinian territories.[15] She describes the Israeli occupation as a "high-speed and high-tech version of the colonization of American Indian homelands."[16] An example she provides is the comparison between the experience of the Dakota people and the Sheikh Jarrah neighborhood in Jerusalem. In both cases, governments used legal tactics to physically erase Indigenous people from their lands. However, Waziyatawin also notes that co-solidarity involves learning from differences. She was inspired by the active resistance of Palestinians, which contrasted with the current responses of her own Lakota people to ongoing colonization: "Given the similar processes of invasion, occupation and colonization, what is striking is not that our Peoples have similarly suffered, but that in the twenty-first century our responses to the suffering are so vastly different."[17]

These examples demonstrate that co-solidarity can take different forms, from identifying shared experiences of oppression to learning from each other's resistance strategies, while acknowledging the unique aspects of each context. This multifaceted approach allows for a more comprehensive form of solidarity that goes beyond simple comparisons, enabling participants to draw inspiration from each other's

---

15. Ali Abunimah, "After Witnessing Palestine's Apartheid, Indigenous and Women of Color Feminists Endorse BDS," The Electronic Intifada, August 3, 2015, https://electronicintifada.net/blogs/ali-abunimah/after-witnessing-palestines-apartheid-indigenous-and-women-color-feminists. See also Krebs and Olwan, "From Jerusalem to the Grand River," 159.

16. Waziyatawin, "Malice Enough in Their Hearts," 172.

17. Waziyatawin, "Malice Enough in Their Hearts," 184.

struggles while respecting specific historical, cultural, and political circumstances.

Biblical Weaponization and Colonial Theology: Shared Histories of Resistance

Despite increased public demonstrations of solidarity, such expressions remain infrequent within Christian discourse. In examining Palestinian and North American Indigenous understandings of land, theological discussions rarely progress beyond acknowledging shared experiences of settler colonialism.[18] Scholars from both contexts challenge dominant Western theological interpretations that have disrupted their relationship with the land. Their focus has primarily been on countering a Western weaponization of theology — shown as Manifest Destiny in North America and Zionist ideology in Israel — that has been used to legitimize exclusive land-ownership claims while simultaneously delegitimizing Indigenous and Palestinian connections to their ancestral territories. Understandably, then, a significant portion of theological work from these communities has been dedicated to resisting the appropriation and misuse of biblical texts that have been wielded against them.[19]

---

18. Shadia Qubti, "A Theological Conversation between Palestinian and North American Indigenous Understandings of Land," UBC Community and Partner Publications, March 31, 2023, http://dx.doi.org/10.14288/1.0444154, 58–60, 47–48.

19. The following works challenge dominant interpretations, reframe biblical narratives from a Palestinian perspective, and assert Palestinian rights and dignity within a theological framework. Munther Isaac's "From Land to Lands, from Eden to the Renewed Earth" (PhD diss., ProQuest Dissertations & Theses, 2014) provides a Christ-centered biblical theology of the promised land. Yohanna Katanacho's *The Land of Christ: A Palestinian Cry* (Woodland Hills, CA: Pickwick Publications, 2013) contributes to evangelical Palestinian theology. Elias Chacour's *Blood Brothers* (Lincoln, NE: Chosen Books, 1985) and *We Belong to the Land* (South Bend, IN: University of Notre Dame Press,

The parallel experiences of Indigenous peoples in North America and Palestinians in relation to biblical interpretation and colonialism are strikingly evident in the works of Robert Allan Warrior (Osage) and Naim Ateek. Their 1989 critiques of liberation theology's interpretation of the Exodus narrative mark one of the earliest theological conversations bridging these two contexts. Samuel Kuruvilla drew connections between Warrior's and Ateek's works, highlighting the ongoing importance of these parallel critiques in understanding and challenging the theological underpinnings of colonialism in both North America and Palestine.[20]

Warrior's influential essay "Canaanites, Cowboys and Indians" critically examines the application of liberation theology to the Native American context.[21] He exposes the dual nature of God in the Exodus story: as both the conqueror of the Canaanites and the deliverer of the Israelites. Warrior argues that readers who identify with the liberated Israelites inadvertently align themselves with the conquer-

---

1990) offer personal narratives intertwined with theological reflections. Rafiq Khoury co-edited *The Basic Document: Theology and Local Church in the Holy Land* (Jerusalem: Al-Liqa Center, first published 1987, 3rd ed. 2015), while Michel Sabbah's *Faithful Witness* (Hyde Park, NY: New City Press, 2009) addresses reconciliation and peace. Geries S. Khoury's *The Intifada of Heaven and the Intifada of Earth* (Nazareth: Al-Hakim Printing Press, 1989 [Arabic]) presents a Palestinian liberation theology.

20. Kuruvilla studies the development of liberation and contextual theology in Israel-Palestine while addressing its historical, political, theological, ideological, and international context. See Samuel J. Kuruvilla, *Radical Christianity in Palestine and Israel: Liberation and Theology in the Middle East* (London: Tauris Academic Studies, 2013), 124–25.

21. Allan Warrior, "Canaanites, Cowboys and Indians," was first published in *Christianity and Crisis* in 1989. The same article was republished in James Treat's *Native and Christian: Indigenous Voices on Religious Identity in the United States and Canada* (New York: Routledge, 1996); and in R. S. Sugirathajah's *Voices from the Margins: Interpreting the Bible in the Third World,* 3rd ed. (Maryknoll, NY: Orbis Books, 2006). See Robert Allen Warrior, "Canaanites, Cowboys, and Indians," *Christianity and Crisis* 49, no. 12 (1989): 21–26.

ing God of the Canaanites. This critique is deeply informed by Warrior's experiences in Israel in 1985 and 1986, where he directly engaged with Palestinian struggles and people, including Ateek.[22] He recalls, "I started by being on the ground there; I got to know a lot of young people and the thing that they were up against in trying to make their own world better. It's just heartbreaking to me."[23] Warrior's analysis culminates in a powerful parallel, when he personifies the voices of the world's Canaanites as those of Indigenous people in Osage County and Wounded Knee and as the cries of Palestinians in Nablus and Gaza. This comparison is particularly poignant given that Manifest Destiny rhetoric often referred to North American Indigenous peoples as Canaanites to delegitimize their claims.

Ateek's *Justice and Only Justice,* the first expression of Palestinian liberation theology, offers a complementary critique from a Palestinian Christian perspective. Like Warrior, Ateek challenges the traditional interpretation of the Exodus narrative that has been used to justify Palestinian displacement. Both theologians seek to reclaim biblical narratives in ways that support the rights and dignity of oppressed peoples. Ateek argues, "The Exodus and the conquest of Canaan are, in the mind of many people, a unified and inseparable theme. For to need an exodus, one must have a promised land. To choose the motif of conquest of the promised land is to invite the need for the oppression, assimilation, control, or dispossession of the indigenous population."[24] This misuse

---

22. Warrior later studied under Edward Said, who was influential on his work on postcolonialism and Indigenous sovereignty. See Kuruvilla, *Radical Christianity,* 124.

23. J. Kēhaulani Kauanui and Robert Allen Warrior, *Speaking of Indigenous Politics: Conversations with Activists, Scholars, and Tribal Leaders* (Minneapolis: University of Minnesota Press, 2018), 339.

24. Naim Stifan Ateek, *Justice and Only Justice: A Palestinian Theology of Liberation* (Maryknoll, NY: Orbis Books, 2002), 80–81.

of the story, Ateek contends, can perpetuate a cycle wherein the liberated become oppressors. Both theologians seek to reclaim biblical narratives in ways that support the rights and dignity of oppressed peoples.

Mark Charles, Soong-Chan Rah, and Steven Salaita similarly expose the intertwined theological justifications for colonization in the United States and Israel. They argue that both nations employ biblical "chosenness" language and the concept of "promised land" to legitimize the displacement of Indigenous peoples and Palestinians. The Doctrine of Discovery, conflated with biblical narratives, has been used to frame colonization and genocide as divine mandates in both contexts. Charles and Rah point to historical examples like John Winthrop's 1630 sermon and contemporary instances such as Netanyahu's 2015 speech to the U.S. Congress, which reveal a shared rhetoric of exceptionalism and divine right to land.[25] This creates a codependent relationship wherein the United States uses Israel's biblical legacy to justify its historical actions, while Israel relies on U.S. support to validate its current policies. Salaita's concept of "Holy Land mentality" further illuminates how this theological framework, originating in American colonization, was later applied to Zionist ideology in Palestine.[26] By associating Indigenous

---

25. John Winthrop was a Puritan pastor who served as the governor of Massachusetts on and off from 1629 to 1949. His famous sermon "A Modell of Christian Charity" shows the understanding of chosenness and the legacy of promised lands that is closely aligned with the Doctrine of Discovery's worldview. See Mark Charles and Soong-Chan Rah, *Unsettling Truths: The Ongoing, Dehumanizing Legacy of the Doctrine of Discovery* (Downers Grove, IL: InterVarsity Press, 2019), 72.

26. Salaita's work examines parallels between Palestinian and Anishinaabe literature, highlighting shared colonial experiences. He uses Hilton Obenzinger's analysis in *American Palestine* to compare American views of the Holy Land with Zionist ideology. See Steven Salaita, *The Holy Land in Transit* (Syracuse, NY: Syracuse University Press, 2006), 23.

peoples and Palestinians with biblical "others," this trans-atlantic colonial theology continues to influence policies and attitudes, justifying ongoing dispossession and oppression in both contexts.

The enduring relevance of these critiques is starkly evident in recent events. On October 28, 2023, three weeks after the Hamas attack, Israeli Prime Minister Benjamin Netanyahu addressed soldiers preparing to enter Gaza, invoking a controversial biblical passage: "Remember what Amalek has done to you, says our Holy Bible."[27] This verse evokes a divine command in 1 Samuel 15:3 for the Israelites to utterly destroy the Amalekites, leaving nothing alive. In this passage, Saul is commanded to destroy all that Amalek has, and do not spare him, "but put to death both man and woman, child and infant, ox and sheep, camel and donkey." Raheb, among others, has pointed out how Netanyahu's use of this text perpetuates a dangerous pattern of biblical weaponization.[28] It simultaneously asserts Israeli claims to the land while dehumanizing and demonizing Palestinians, effectively casting them in the role of the Amalekites—a people divinely marked for destruction. This modern instance chillingly mirrors the historical misuse of the same biblical narrative against Indigenous peoples in North America. In the late

27. Address by the prime minister of Israel, 28 October 2023, https://www.youtube.com/watch?v=lIPkoDk6isc. Translation: "Israel-Hamas war: 'We Will Fight and We Will Win', says Benjamin Netanyahu," Sky News (28 October 2023), https://news.sky.com/video/israel-hamas-war-we-will-fight-and-we-will-win-says-benjamin-netanyahu-1299 5212.

28. Yonat Shimron, "As Court Decides on Genocide Charge, Netanyahu's Use of a Bible Passage Haunts Him," Religion News Service, January 25, 2024, https://religionnews.com/2024/01/25/as-court-decides-on-genocide-charge-netanyahus-use-of-a-bible-passage-haunts-him/; "Video: Decolonizing Palestine: The Land, the People, the Bible," Religion and Public Life at Harvard Divinity School, June 18, 2024, https://rpl.hds.harvard.edu/news/2024/06/18/video-decolonizing-palestine-land-people-bible.

nineteenth century, this very association with the Amalekites was used to justify atrocities such as the massacre of Native Americans at Wounded Knee in 1890.[29]

The parallels between these historical and contemporary misuses of Scripture are striking. They exemplify the exact dynamic that Warrior and Ateek identified decades ago: the portrayal of God as both liberator of one group and conqueror of another. This cyclical weaponization of biblical text — from justifying the genocide of Indigenous peoples in North America to that of Palestinians today — underscores the urgent need to critically examine and challenge such interpretations. It demonstrates how colonial and settler-colonial ideologies continue to exploit religious narratives to justify oppression and territorial expansion, making the work of theologians such as Warrior and Ateek as relevant today as it was over three decades ago.

The persistence of this ideology is evident in current American political discourse, notably in the resistance to calls for a ceasefire in Gaza. This contemporary example underscores the enduring influence of such theological-political narratives in shaping policy and public opinion, revealing deep-seated connections between American and Israeli approaches to Indigenous land rights and conflicts. Additionally, in the Call to Repentance, Palestinian theologians highlight how colonial biblical interpretations that once justified violence against Indigenous peoples now legitimize Palestinian displacement. The same theological framework that rationalized historical atrocities is evident in contemporary justifications of violence against Palestinians, often framed as "self-defense."[30]

---

29. John Corrigan and Lynn S. Neal, eds., *Religious Intolerance in America: A Documentary History* (Chapel Hill: University of North Carolina Press, 2010), 128.

30. "A Call for Repentance: An Open Letter from Palestinian Christians to Western Church Leaders and Theologians," Kairos Pales-

The aforementioned discourse elucidates the theological frameworks of conquest that have co-opted biblical texts for political objectives. However, the exposed parallels predominantly focus on the interconnections and dynamics among colonizing powers, specifically the American, Canadian, and Israeli systems of control. These analyses primarily address and emphasize the position of Palestinians and Indigenous peoples as colonized subjects. While scholars acknowledge the distinctiveness of these settler-colonial processes, despite their similarities, the preponderance of attention is directed toward situating oneself in relation to these dominant powers and ideologies. Consequently, in attempting to explore the potential for co-learning conversations in these contexts, a critical question emerges: Is there scope for Palestinians and Indigenous peoples of Turtle Island to engage with each other beyond their shared status as colonized populations? This inquiry seeks to transcend the binary of colonizer-colonized and explore the potential for dialogue and mutual understanding that is not solely predicated on their experiences of subjugation.

Beyond Critique: Creating Space for Palestinian-Indigenous Theological Dialogue

The need for conversation beyond critiquing dominant theologies between Palestinian and North American Indigenous contexts stems from their distinct historical experiences and theological approaches. While both face settler-colonial challenges, they are at different stages of colonization and have developed varied strategies for self-determination and resistance. Their approaches to knowledge systems, activism, and

tine, October 20, 2023, https://www.kairospalestine.ps/index.php/resources/statements/a-call-for-repentance-an-open-letter-from-pal estinian-christians-to-western-church-leaders-and-theologians.

theological discourse differ significantly, with Indigenous theologians often focusing on preserving traditional knowledge and Palestinians seeking to foster alliances for change. These differences, if not addressed, risk limiting meaningful dialogue between the two groups. However, engaging in conversation beyond critique offers rich potential for mutual learning and solidarity. It could allow for the exchange of resistance strategies, methods of cultural preservation, and approaches to land-based theologies. Such dialogue could lead to more comprehensive and nuanced understandings of land, spirituality, and relationships with creation, incorporating insights from both contexts. Ultimately, by moving beyond critique to constructive dialogue, theologians from both backgrounds could develop more inclusive and effective approaches to addressing their unique challenges while fostering meaningful co-solidarity.

One of those conversations that paves a space to further such dialogue is Andrea Smith's "Land and People" in Mae Cannon's *A Land Full of God*. Smith's analysis of the Israeli-Palestinian conflict challenges the notion that one group of people has a greater entitlement to land than another, a premise often embedded in the concept of a nation-state. She traces this idea back to Western notions of land ownership, mainly how Christians interpret Scriptures through the lens of God, land, and people. Smith proposes Indigenous perspectives that offer an alternative to the Western view of land ownership and emphasizes the importance of Christians not only to decolonize their theologies but also their imaginations.[31]

Smith's reflections open up a novel space for dialogue between Palestinians and Indigenous peoples of Turtle

---

31. Andrea Smith, "Land and People," in *A Land Full of God: Christian Perspectives on the Holy Land*, ed. Mae Elise Cannon (Eugene, OR: Cascade Books, 2017), 89–98 (94–95).

Island, one that transcends the traditional colonizer-colonized binary and challenges conventional notions of liberation. This dialogue space invites participants to reimagine their relationships with land, sovereignty, and one another. The reconsideration of the concept of nationhood is central to this dialogue. Smith envisions an inclusive nationhood built on interconnected understanding between nations, rather than exclusive control over land. This approach calls for a radical re-orientation toward a relationship to land, in which "all are welcome to live on the land" and people understand themselves as cohabitants rather than controllers of creation.[32] The dialogue encourages a critical examination of the assumed relationship between peoples and land and questions the notion that the ultimate goal of any liberation struggle is the attainment of a nation-state. It challenges participants to imagine liberation not as a zero-sum game but as a process that necessitates the well-being of all peoples. This space also invites a re-examination of biblical and theological understandings. Smith's evolution from equating support for Jewish people with support for the modern State of Israel to a more nuanced view exemplifies the kind of theological reflection this dialogue could foster. It encourages participants to consider how religious texts and beliefs can be interpreted to support inclusive, rather than exclusive, claims to land and resources.

The dialogue also prompts a critical look at solidarity movements. Smith critiques those who base their solidarity with Palestinians on the assumption that Indigenous people in the United States have already "vanished," highlighting the need for a more holistic approach to justice that does not accept the expendability of any group.[33]

Importantly, this dialogue space calls for a "decoloniza-

---

32. Smith, "Land and People," 91–92.
33. Smith, "Land and People," 96.

tion of our imaginations." It challenges participants not merely to envision justice in worldly terms but to consider "what God considers to be justice," and to believe in "a God of the (im)possible."[34] This approach opens up new possibilities for understanding liberation and justice that go beyond current dominant political and social paradigms. While Smith's reflections on land and indigeneity provide valuable insights, her understanding of the Palestinian situation was initially limited and based on biblical interpretations rather than direct engagement with Palestinian experiences or writings.

Reimagining Land and Liberation:
Insights from Indigenous–Palestinian Dialogue

Building upon Andrea Smith's call for decolonizing theology and reimagining our hermeneutical approaches, I recognized the need to create a space for my own epistemological reimagination of theological discourse. This led me to conceptualize a contrapuntal dialogue between a Palestinian and a North American Indigenous theologian — "The Bible and Land Colonization" by Mitri Raheb and "The Land Takes Care of Us: Recovering Creator's Relational Design" by Daniel Zacharias.[35] To embark on this methodological trajectory, I found it imperative to critically examine my own positionality and scholarly motivations. This necessitated grappling with fundamental questions of academic praxis: What are my research objectives? Who constitutes my intended readership? Whose voices do I prioritize in my scholarly discourse? Re-examining these questions became crucial in forging this new path of theological engagement.

---

34. Smith, "Land and People," 97.
35. Both texts are chapters in K. K. Yeo and Gene L. Green, eds., *Theologies of Land: Contested Land, Spatial Justice, and Identity* (Eugene, OR: Cascade Books, 2021).

This process of reflexive analysis and conceptual reimagination enabled me to approach the contrapuntal reading of Raheb's and Zacharias's works with a renewed hermeneutical lens, one that seeks to honor both traditions while creating a discursive space for new, decolonial epistemologies to emerge.[36]

Additionally, reading their texts contrapuntally, for me, transcends traditional colonizer-colonized narratives. This space invites a critical reexamination of fundamental concepts such as land possession, inheritance, and the relationship between people and land. Similar to the work of Smith, the exploration of land-based theologies that challenge Western notions of land as a commodity is central to this dialogue. Raheb's vision of an inclusive Palestinian identity as rightful inheritors of the land can be put into conversation with Zacharias's concept of humanity belonging to the land rather than possessing it.[37] This juxtaposition opens up possibilities for reimagining relationships to land that are neither exploitative nor exclusive. The dialogue space encourages

---

36. A contrapuntal reading, developed by Edward Said, is a methodological approach that juxtaposes two different texts or perspectives, allowing them to interact and inform each other without seeking to find common ground or harmonize their differences. This method aims to explore new meanings that emerge from reading texts together rather than comparing them for similarities. It acknowledges the distinct voices and contexts of each text while revealing shared themes and divergent viewpoints. The approach emphasizes the reader's perspective and the process of juxtaposition rather than predetermined outcomes. See Qubti, "A Theological Conversation," 58–60.

37. Raheb presents an inclusive and historically grounded understanding of Palestinian identity. He asserts, "The Palestinian people (Muslims, Christians, Jews, and Samaritans) with a significant continuity from biblical times until the present are the native people who survived empires and occupations." Raheb emphasizes the dynamic nature of this identity, noting that it has shifted through various historical periods—from Canaanite and Philistine, to Judahite and Israelite, to Hasmonean, Roman, Byzantine, Arab, Ottoman, and finally to Palestinian (Qubti, "A Theological Conversation," 70).

a deeper understanding of the spiritual dimensions of land relationships. Zacharias's insights on the spiritual impact of landlessness on both colonized and colonizer can enrich Raheb's focus on physical land loss. This could lead to discussions on how to reconnect with land-based spiritualities and fulfill sacred responsibilities to the land, even in contexts of displacement or occupation.

An important aspect of this dialogue is the integration of different worldviews and knowledge systems. Raheb's juggling of time-based and place-based perspectives can be explored alongside Zacharias's emphasis on Indigenous place-based understandings.[38] This interchange could foster a more comprehensive approach to land theology that honors both historical continuity and specific geographical contexts. The space also invites a collaborative effort to decolonize biblical interpretations. By bringing together Raheb's postcolonial critique of Western theologies and Zacharias's intercultural reading, which draws on Indigenous knowledge systems, participants can work toward new, more inclusive ways of interpreting sacred texts.

Critical Reflections: Limitations and Future Directions in Palestinian Theology

Crucially, this dialogue acknowledges the different stages of colonization experienced by Palestinians and Indigenous

---

38. Land-based understanding in Indigenous cultures emphasizes place over time. As Josiah Baker explains in "Native American Contributions to a Christian Theology of Space," Indigenous theology focuses on where spiritual realities manifest in specific locations, contrasting with Western theology's emphasis on when. This approach reinforces Indigenous peoples' covenantal relationship with their lands and reflects a holistic worldview connecting spiritual and physical realms. See Josiah Baker, "Native American Contributions to a Christian Theology of Space," *Studies in World Christianity* 22, no. 3 (2016): 234–46, https://doi.org/10.3366/swc.2016.0158.

peoples of Turtle Island. It recognizes that, while there are similarities in their experiences, there are also significant differences in their current realities and the challenges they face. This awareness can lead to more nuanced and context-specific theological reflections and solidarity efforts. The dialogue space also grapples with the tension between academic discourse and activism. It explores how theological insights can inform and be informed by on-the-ground realities and resistance movements, seeking a balance between theoretical reflection and practical action.

Furthermore, this space encourages discussions on varying concepts of self-determination. It puts Indigenous efforts to reclaim ways of being and knowing into conversation with Palestinian pursuits of land rights and statehood, seeking areas of common ground and mutual support. And lastly, the dialogue incorporates reflections on ecological responsibility, drawing on both Palestinian and Indigenous perspectives on human relationships with the natural world. This aspect recognizes the interconnectedness of all creation and the shared responsibility in the community of creation.

This exploration of North American Indigenous and Palestinian theological perspectives on land and colonization offers profound insights that address the key questions posed at the outset. The lessons gleaned from North American Indigenous theologians, who have experienced settler colonialism and genocide long before the Palestinian people, provide valuable frameworks for understanding and challenging similar processes in the Palestinian context. Their critiques of dominant theological narratives and emphasis on land-based spirituality offer rich avenues for reimagining Palestinian relationships to land beyond Western nation-state models.

Crucially, this dialogue prompts a reconsideration of what a decolonial meaning for Palestinian connection to land might entail, particularly for those in diaspora. As a Palestinian residing in Canada, I have come to understand that my relationship to Palestinian land is ever-present, expressed through the ongoing practice of culture and traditions rooted in sacred wisdom about our relationship with the creator. This perspective offers a way to maintain a profound connection to land even in contexts of displacement. Moreover, this exploration has led me to confront my dual positionality: being displaced due to one settler-colonial state while residing on stolen lands in another. This complex reality shapes my contextual theology and understanding of my place in the world, adding layers of nuance to the dialogue between Palestinian and Indigenous theologies.

Ultimately, this multifaceted conversation opens up new possibilities for solidarity, resistance, and healing that go beyond critique of dominant powers. It envisions more just and sustainable futures for all peoples and the lands they inhabit, while acknowledging the complexities of displacement and the ongoing responsibilities we hold to both our ancestral lands and the lands we currently inhabit. This dialogue not only enriches our theological understanding but also challenges us to embody these insights in our daily lives and struggles for justice.

Conclusion: From Parallel Roots to Shared Growth

Noticing sumac in Vancouver serves as a powerful metaphor for my research journey. Just as sumac has always been present in both Palestine and North America, the connections between Palestinian and Indigenous experiences have always existed. However, my eyes were opened to see these parallels only through my engagement with Indigenous contexts in Canada. Like the sumac tree, rooted in both landscapes, the shared experiences of colonization and resistance have been ever-present, waiting to be recognized.

This process of recognition mirrors the broader implications of this research. By engaging deeply with Indigenous
perspectives, I have not only gained new insights into the
Palestinian struggle but also uncovered connections that
were always there, yet previously unseen. This realization
underscores the importance of dialogue and the potential for
mutual understanding and solidarity that can emerge when
we open ourselves to new perspectives. Just as the sumac
tree has adapted to thrive in diverse environments while
maintaining its essential nature, Palestinian theology can
draw strength from Indigenous insights while remaining
true to its roots. This metaphor encapsulates the potential
for a decolonial Palestinian theology that is both grounded
in its own context and enriched by solidarity with other colonized peoples. The sumac, once merely a nostalgic sight, is
a living testament to the interconnectedness of our struggles
and the potential for mutual learning. It reminds me that,
sometimes, the most profound insights are already present
in our environment. We just need new perspectives to truly
see and understand them.

7

Palestinian Theology of Martyrdom

JOHN S. MUNAYER AND SAMUEL S. MUNAYER
Jerusalem and al-Lydd

> The Christian must prepare him- and herself to witness
> to his and her faith, either by the reality of submitting
> to a daily life that is difficult or even by sacrificing his
> or her life.   —Michel Sabbah[1]

Since October 7, 2023, thousands of lives have been brutally
taken across our land: men, women, and children. While settler colonialism has shaped the Palestinian experience for
generations, what we now witness is unprecedented: the
deliberate destruction of a people, namely, genocide.[2] Just as
Christ was crucified by the hands of an empire determined
to maintain its dominance, thousands of Palestinians are
publicly executed to sustain the life of today's empire. Gaza

---

1. Michel Sabbah, "Pastoral Letter of His Beatitude Patriarch
Michel Sabbah Latin Patriarch of Jerusalem," Vatican, 2008, https://
https://www.vatican.va/roman_curia/institutions_connected/
oessh/oessh_20080301_sabbah_pastoral-letter_en.html.

2. To further understand the term and the accusation against Israel,
see ICJ, "Application of the Convention on the Prevention and Punishment of the Crime of Genocide in the Gaza Strip (South Africa v.
Israel)," Order of 26 January 2024, I.C.J. Reports 2024, https://www.
icj-cij.org/case/192.

has become a symbol of death, a "graveyard for children."[3] For those of us outside Gaza, Zionist violence reaches unprecedented levels across historical Palestine. Amid this onslaught, a painful question haunts many Palestinians, especially the youth: "Do we remain in our homeland, or do we leave and seek an easier life elsewhere?"

This was a question we asked ourselves as a family in October 2023. The conversation began because some of our family members received death threats by a Jerusalem-based Israeli right-wing organization. This organization was looking for our family members to "destroy them."[4] That event felt like the closest parallel to what our grandparents endured during the Nakba, when they were forcibly displaced from their homes in the city of al-Lydd. We found ourselves consumed by questions: What would we do if someone came to take our home? Could we ever bring ourselves to leave if a threat appeared at our doorstep?

This incident reflects a broader pattern within Israeli society, one that seeks not only to exact revenge on Palestinians for the October 7 attack, but also to intimidate and violently suppress those who oppose Zionism and advocate for liberative reconciliation. Within this context, woven into our shared experiences and personal family stories, we encountered the profound intersection of death, life, and meaning, all embodied in the concept of Christian martyrdom. In this encounter, faith undergoes a profound transformation, as faith in Christ provided a framework to understand martyrs and martyrdom. Simultaneously, the killing of many illuminated and reshaped the understanding of Scripture, Christian tradition, and theological reflection. In this dynamic

---

3. UNICEF, "Gaza Has Become a Graveyard for Thousands of Children," 2023, https://www.unicef.org/press-releases/gaza-has-become-graveyard-thousands-children.

4. The phrase used by a member of the organization.

relationship, the martyrs of today and Christ become interpreters of each other.

Martyrdom in Palestine is not merely a reflection of past narratives of sacrifice, but an ongoing lived reality, deeply embedded in daily experiences.[5] The term is frequently invoked in both religious and political contexts, shaping the terms of discourse. Palestinian consciousness is steeped in the presence of martyrs, whether immortalized through graffiti on the walls of refugee camps, honored in mosques, or venerated as saints in churches. However, for some, martyrdom represents a troubling glorification of suffering that veers dangerously toward sacrificialism.[6] For others, it carries negative connotations in contemporary times, often linked to acts of "terrorism" labeled as martyrdom.[7] Indeed, the definition of martyrdom is contested, evoking various meanings for different people.

Even when theologians engage with martyrdom and reflect on martyrs themselves, such as Oscar Romero, Dietrich Bonhoeffer, Martin Luther King Jr., and Shireen Abu Akleh, to name a few, it lacks deep analysis of the broader realities of martyrdom, particularly in contexts of ongoing genocide. As a result, martyrdom is rarely explored with the seriousness it warrants in theological forums despite its pervasive presence in daily life. In short, the reality of martyrdom demands critical attention, especially in efforts to conceptualize theology in the face of genocide. Truly, not engaging with martyrdom in Palestinian theology is to deny a fundamental reality and, thus, to mislead in the path of discipleship and liberation, since martyrdom comes about as

---

5. Sabeel Center, "Palestinian Christian Witness," in *Introduction into Palestinian Theology*, ed. Munther Isaac (Dyar Bethlehem, 2017), 23. Translation from Arabic by the authors.

6. Jon Sobrino, *Witnesses to the Kingdom: The Martyrs of El Salvador and the Crucified Peoples* (New York: Orbis Books, 2003).

7. Sobrino, *Witnesses to the Kingdom*.

a consequence of liberatory praxis as a follower of Christ. As Rafiq Khoury states, "Tell me the Christ in whom you believe, and I will tell you the kind of Christian you are."[8] The Christ one follows shapes the way one responds to oppression.

A Palestinian theology of martyrdom aims to offer insights into the call to bear witness to Christ in times of genocide, to address the challenge martyrdom presents to the church, and to sustain hope during suffering. This chapter begins by defining and examining martyrdom through Scripture and Christian tradition. These insights are then contextualized within the current reality in Palestine, seeking to contribute to the witness of God's love amid genocide. Ultimately, this chapter aspires to place martyrdom at the heart of Palestinian theological reflection, uncovering the good news of Christ and proclaiming it to the victims of history.[9]

Martyrdom in Scripture

Christian Scripture is full of theological references and content concerning martyrdom, but, in this short section, we will examine some basic biblical meanings in the New Testament.[10] The word "martyr" comes from Greek: "to be a witness." This term comes from mostly legal contexts, in which someone testifies or is a witness in court. Similarly, the word martyr in Arabic is shaheed, which also means "witness" and also bears legal connotations. In other words, a theology

---

8. Rafiq Khoury, *Incarnation of Eastern Churches in the Arab Tent: Approaches from the Palestinian Perspective* (Bethlehem: Al-Liqa Publishing, 1998), 27. Translation from Arabic by the authors.

9. Rafiq Khoury, *Palestinian Contextual Theology (1067–2019)* (Jerusalem: Al-Liqa, 2019), 213. The book centers Palestinian theology as the theology of the oppressed. Translation from Arabic by the authors.

10. While the Old Testament also engages in this concept, because of space we will focus on the New Testament.

of martyrdom can be better described as a theology of witness amidst trial. But to what/whom is one bearing witness? How does one bear witness? What is the trial? And who is on trial?

In the four Gospels, the theme of bearing witness is central, especially in the Gospel of John, which opens with the concept of bearing witness to the light.[11] John the Baptist's main vocation is described: "He came as a witness to testify concerning that light" (1:7). The light being Jesus Christ, who "out of his fullness . . . all received grace in place of grace already given" (1:16). This is central to John the Baptist's ministry, bearing witness to Christ and recognizing this transformative moment (John 1:19–36). Likewise, the Gospel of John also ends with John the Beloved's testimony of Christ: "this is the disciple who testifies to these things and who wrote them down" (John 21:24). It suggests that being a disciple of Jesus is embodying the role of a witness to God's liberating grace and love.

If we are to be witnesses to the truth of Jesus, then Christ is the one who is on trial. As can be seen in the other three Gospels as well, Jesus is constantly tested, accused, doubted, and testified against by teachers, scribes, and leaders (Matthew 16:1; Mark 8:11; Mark 3:2; Luke 6:7); beginning in his ministry in Galilee and, finally, in the court in Jerusalem where he is crucified (Mark 14:53–15:15). In fact, Jesus warns that, like him, his followers will have to literally be witnesses in courts and in front of kings and governors (Mark 13:9; Luke 21:12–17). The Synoptic Gospels make sure to place Peter's test in a central position that echoes the testing of all disciples. It is no coincidence that the phrasing of the denial is in legal terms.[12]

---

11. Allison A. Trites, "The Idea of Witness in the Synoptic Gospels—Some Juridical Considerations," *Themelios* 5 (1968): 18–26 (18).

12. Trites, "The Idea of Witness," 21.

No doubt, the call to deny oneself, pick up one's cross, and follow Jesus is not to be taken lightly. It is at the center of the Gospel of Mark (8:34), and it should be the foundation of Christian discipleship. For if we truly follow Jesus, it will lead to similar trials (Matthew 16:24–26). Jesus's call is not centered on numbers of followers or physically/financially surviving as a community but bearing witness to the Kingdom of God. Interestingly, the call to bear witness is not an individual one alone, but always in community. Witness is to be practiced in and through deep relationships with others, as the whole body of Christ together. We are called to be salt and light as a community, even at a high price.

With that said, Jesus being on trial seems to be temporary, as his condemnation will be overturned through his resurrection (Ephesians 1:20–21). And the people who are on trial in light of Christ's glorification are the people exposed to Christ and the ministry: "But whoever disowns me before others, I will disown before my Father in heaven" (Matthew 10:33). The disciples themselves are actually instructed to bear witness to those who do not recognize the good news of the Christ moment (Luke 9:5; Mark 6:11). As such, Jesus moves from being the condemned to being the judge, from accused to praised, from being on trial to bearing witness (Matthew 25:31).

In the same way that followers of Christ are to bear witness to him, Jesus promises to be their witness on judgment day (Matthew 10:32). Thus, the tables are turned. If Jesus and his followers are judged by earthly judges, they will later be vindicated as Christ will become both judge and a witness to humanity. A brief examination of the concept of witness in the Gospels reveals that it is a central vocation for those who identify as Christians.

We see the same theme of witness in the Book of Acts. In the first chapter, as Christ is about to ascend into heaven and foretells the coming of the Holy Spirit, the main task for the disciples is to "be my [Jesus's] witnesses in Jerusalem, and in all Judea and Samaria, and to the ends of the earth" (Acts 1:8). Here, like in the Gospels, the call to bear witness is in community; a call that the early church carries out in the Book of Acts. Moreover, the main criterion for choosing the twelfth disciple to replace Judas is someone who was "with us the whole time the Lord Jesus was living among us," including being a "witness" to the resurrection (Acts 1:21–22). This mission of being witnesses to Christ is carried out by the apostles, and central to Paul's calling: "You will be his witness to all people" (Acts 22:15).

The concept of witness and judicial language runs throughout the New Testament and is central in the last composition, in the Book of Revelation. The whole book is a "testimony" to what John experienced: "He made it known by sending his angel to his servant John, who testifies to everything he saw — that is, the word of God and the testimony of Jesus Christ" (Revelation 1:1–2). The very criterion of the faithful in the book is being steadfast witnesses to the testimony of Jesus Christ (Revelation 12:11, 17; 17:6; 20:4). It is also the identifying marker of being part of the family of Jesus Christ, "I am a fellow servant with you and with your brothers and sisters who hold to the testimony of Jesus" (Revelation 19:10). This family, or body of Christ, is to be met with violent and tempting challenges that may cost them their lives. The book is there to encourage and bless the faithful witnesses (Revelation 1:3), who may or may not die in the process. Indeed, the witnesses who were killed are placed under the altar and call on God to bring justice (Revelation 6:9–10). Perhaps we can hear this call from the suffering people of Gaza today.

Martyrdom in Tradition

The theme of being a witness, a martyr, continues from the New Testament and the early church to the Christian tradition, and indeed the Palestinian Christian tradition today. The various persecutions and hostilities that the Jesus movement faced in its early stages solidified and centralized the importance of martyrs. One would expect that suffering would be a core element of a movement that emerged at a time of great instability in Palestine, in tension with Second Temple Judaism, and worshiped a convicted criminal of the Roman Empire.[13] While martyrdom did not always refer to Christians who were killed due to their witness, the intense killing and persecution of Christians, starting with Stephen, made a more conceptual connection between martyrdom and being killed.[14]

There are many aspects one could analyze from the long and rich tradition of martyrdom in the Christian faith. But, for this chapter, we will focus on the idea that one can be martyred for action as well as belief. While there are different positions concerning the extent to which Christians were relentlessly persecuted in the first three centuries,[15] it is certain that various emperors and other regional Roman officials intentionally persecuted Christians to various degrees, creating "an irregular rhythm in the outbreaks of persecution."[16]

Nevertheless, and perhaps more crucial, besides official persecution for someone's belief (their personal religious conviction), Christians were persecuted as a result of their actions, according to various historians. This is reflected by

---

13. Paul Middleton, *Radical Martyrdom and Cosmic Conflict in Early Christianity* (London: T. & T. Clark, 2006), 1.

14. Matthew D. Lundberg, *Christian Martyrdom and Christian Violence: On Suffering and Wielding the Sword* (New York: Oxford University Press, 2021), 9.

15. Candida R. Moss, *The Myth of Persecution: How Early Christians Invented a Story of Martyrdom* (New York: HarperOne, 2014); Rubén Rosario Rodríguez, *Christian Martyrdom and Political Violence: A Comparative Theology with Judaism and Islam* (Cambridge: Cambridge University Press, 2017), 83–123.

16. Rodríguez, *Christian Martyrdom and Political Violence*, 89.

early church fathers, some of whom lived under Roman persecution, such as Gregory of Nazianzus, Ignatius of Antioch, Origen, Polycarp of Smyrna, and others.[17] Correlating to the passage on the impossibility of serving two masters in Matthew 6:24, "Christians . . . could not be good citizens of the Roman Empire. . . . Christian theology and Roman Imperial ideology were meta-narratives competing for the same ground."[18] Christians insisted on worshiping one God, Jesus as King, and participating in the work of the Kingdom of God—an attitude and behavior that were in complete contradiction to the Roman cults that worshiped multiple gods, saw Caesar as lord, and advanced the empire forcefully and violently. Thus, brutal punishments came upon some Christians, as "a Christian who refused to sacrifice to the emperor when called upon to do so was in violation of the law and subject to the extreme penalty."[19]

The emphasis on actions that were in contradiction to the empire's ideology, abusive systems, and violence could be seen as the main reason for the persecution and martyrdom of Christians. One can draw parallels to more contemporary martyrs who paid a similar high price, including with their lives, for acts against empires, such as Dietrich Bonhoeffer, Oscar Romero, Martin Luther King Jr., and Shireen Abu Akleh. Standing for the oppressed and for justice, which is at the heart of the Kingdom of God, seems to be one of the main and most dangerous reasons for martyrdom; whether that be true for the early church or for Christians in Palestine today.

Due to the harsh circumstances Christians lived under for the first few centuries, the theology of martyrdom became

---

17. Byran M. Litfin, *Early Christian Martyr Stories: An Evangelical Introduction with New Translations* (Grand Rapids, MI: Baker Publishing Group, 2014).

18. Middleton, *Radical Martyrdom*, 40.

19. G. Warren Bowersock, *Martyrdom and Rome* (Cambridge: Cambridge University Press, 1995), 25.

prominent and widespread. Often, it was a way to show
one's true obedience and love for God. In fact, publicly self-
identifying as a Christian was used to show that one not
only follows Christ but is in opposition to other theologies/
ideologies.[20] Literature and Scripture concerning martyrdom,
such as the Acts of the Apostles, the Book of Revelation, and
letters between church members, were prominent among
early Christians.[21] They were used to encourage, comfort,
and strengthen a movement that was in contradiction to
the empire. Even after the adoption of Christianity by the
empire itself and the beginning of the official formulation of
the religion, stories of martyrs were encouraged to be told
during festivals, illustrating "a more homogenised orthodoxy of doctrine and practice."[22]

Martyrdom and witness continues to be a discussed
topic in recent times in liberation theology. Liberation
theology sought to challenge the concept of martyrdom
within the church and theology, contextualizing it within
its current events. The works of James H. Cone, Leonardo
Boff, Marcella Althaus-Reid, Rafiq Khoury, Geries Khoury,
Desmond Tutu, Rosemary Radford Ruether, and others
are examples of such work. Notably, Jon Sobrino sought
to redefine martyrdom by broadening its scope beyond the
traditional understanding of dying for faith as an explicit
doctrinal confession. In his view, martyrdom must include
those who give their lives in the pursuit of justice, dignity,
and the defense of the oppressed, even if they are not explicitly killed for their religious beliefs.[23] Sobrino challenged

20. Jane D. McLarty, "Early Christian Theologies of Martyrdom,"
in *The Wiley Blackwell Companion to Christian Martyrdom*, ed. Paul Middleton (Newark, NJ: Wiley, 2020), 120–34 (123).
21. McLarty, "Early Christian Theologies of Martyrdom," 120.
22. Rodríguez, *Christian Martyrdom and Political Violence*, 91.
23. Jon Sobrino, *Principle of Mercy: Taking the Crucified People from
the Cross* (Maryknoll, NY: Orbis Books, 1994).

the church to see martyrdom as a radical and transformative engagement with the world, where faith and action are inseparable.

Furthermore, Sobrino connected martyrdom to the concept of the "suffering church," emphasizing that martyrdom is not an isolated event but deeply rooted in the collective suffering and witness of a community that stands for values of love, mercy, and justice.[24] Thus, the cost of bearing witness is multifaceted, with emotional, social, political, economic, and physical ramifications. Being killed is often the last stage of a martyr, whose painful journey starts at a much earlier stage of life.

In Palestine, this tradition of martyrs continues today in many expressions of the Christian faith. It is common to see Palestinian Christians venerate local saints, such as St. George or St. Barbara, when their stories of martyrdom are told in churches and homes during annual feasts and interpreted dialogically with martyrs of today.[25] Visually, one can see icons of martyrs above, around, and in the homes of Palestinian Christians, giving them a prominent place in their daily lives. Events such as Sabt al-Nour—Saturday of Light in English, also known as Holy Fire—in the Church of Resurrection—also known as Church of the Holy Sepulcher and in the past also named the Church of Witness—emphasize the role of bearing witness to the resurrection and the Kingdom of God.[26] The theological foundation of martyrdom continues to run through the Bible, tradition, land, and

---

24. Sobrino, *Witnesses to the Kingdom*.

25. See Elizabeth Martejin, "Martyrdom, Liberation, and Belonging: An Ethnography on the Popular Saint George Veneration among Palestinian Christians," *Journal of World Christianity* 10, no. 1 (2020): 53–67.

26. Joseph Hazboun and Majdi al-Shomali, eds., *Palestine the Cradle of Christianity* (Bethlehem: Dar al-Kalima, 2024), 15. Translation from Arabic by the authors.

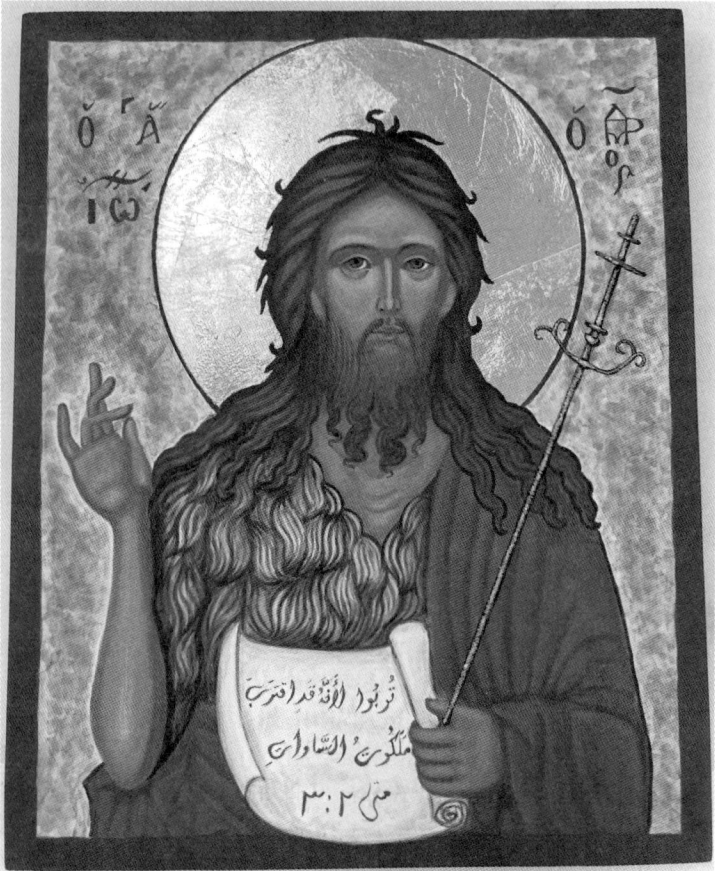

Icon of Saint John the Baptist, written by John S. Munayer in 2024. The scroll reads, in Arabic, "Repent, for the kingdom of heaven has come near" (Matthew 3:2).

people who seek to bear witness to the liberating Christ in Palestine today.

A number of key theological foundations emerge from this short overview of witness in the New Testament and the Christian tradition: (1) Being a Christian means bearing witness to Christ and his Kingdom; (2) while Jesus was and is on trial in earthly courts, we humans will be on trial when the Kingdom is fully consummated; (3) bearing witness as a Christian will be costly in several ways; (4) bearing witness is to be done in community; (5) martyrdom is associated with one's actions for justice.

Insights for Palestinian Theology

The Christian centrality of martyrdom offers critical insights into the current context in Palestine and, more specifically, Palestinian theology. First, witnessing to Christ in times of oppression and understanding the faith of martyrdom directly challenge the "theology of survival" that exists in Palestine. This theology of survival, prevalent among some churches and Palestinian Christians, seeks to address the stark realities of displacement and migration faced by Palestinian Christians. Before 1948, Palestinian Christians constituted a significant portion of the population in historical Palestine, comprising approximately 11 to 12 percent. However, immediately following the Nakba, this number dropped to 8 percent. After the Naksa in 1967, the percentage declined even further, falling to less than 2.4 percent.[27] Today, Palestinian Christians make up less than 2 percent of the population, with projections suggesting a continued decline. In Bethlehem, for instance, Christians once accounted for 86 percent of the population before 1948 but now represent only 12 percent.[28] This decline is most severe in Gaza, where the two-thousand-year presence of Christians faces unprecedented

---

27. Statistics taken from *Palestinian Christians: Emigration, Displacement and Diaspora*, ed. Mitri Raheb (Bethlehem: Diyar Publishing, 2017).

28. Badil (BADIL Resource Center for Palestinian Residency and Refugee Rights) and Kairos Palestine, *Palestinian Christians: The Forcible Displacement and Dispossession Continues* (Bethlehem: Badil Kairos Palestine Publication, 2023).

threats of extinction due to the current mass destruction and extermination.[29]

The sense of community in the First Intifada contrasts sharply with the fragmentation and ongoing migration experienced today. The decline of Palestinian Christians in Palestine represents a profound loss on multiple levels, prompting churches and Palestinian Christian leaders to develop a "theology of survival." While some forms of this theology offer a means of resistance, the version critiqued here focuses on preserving the physical presence of Palestinian Christians and institutions, often at the expense of their mission of witness. This theology of survival frequently becomes the primary narrative shared with international visitors by Palestinian Christian institutions and leaders. Churches in Jerusalem have issued numerous statements warning of the threats to Christian presence in the Holy Land, a concern echoed across the Middle East.[30] These concerns are undeniably legitimate. However, the problem arises when this theology becomes fixated on survival, equating numeric presence with the presence of Christ or the ability of our witness in the land.

One might ask how many church statements bore witness to the plight of the oppressed in Palestine compared to those expressing concern about the presence of Christians in the land. What message does it send when the leaders of the Orthodox, Armenian Apostolic, and Catholic Churches closed the Church of Resurrection in protest against Israel's imposed municipal taxes, yet have kept its doors open since the genocide in Gaza, even as their congregants are killed and their churches damaged by Israeli bombs? This dispar-

29. Alessandra Bajec, "Will Gaza's Palestinian Christian Community Survive Israel's War?" *The New Arab*, 2024, https://www.newarab.com/analysis/will-gazas-christian-community-survive-israels-war.

30. Mitri Raheb, *The Politics of Persecution: Middle Eastern Christians in the Age of Empire* (Waco, TX: Baylor University Press, 2021).

ity suggests a theology that prioritizes self-preservation over the risk of prophetic engagement. With the Christian presence in the land increasingly dwindling and the diaspora growing—a trend that is likely to accelerate—this "theology of survival" risks fostering fatalism. It may reduce our mission to venting about our reality, especially before Western audiences, instead of actively engaging with the broader call to witness, even to the point of ultimate sacrifice.

At times, the fixation on survival has also cultivated sectarian attitudes and Islamophobic sentiments among the Palestinian Christian community against Palestinian Muslims. With the increasing decline of the community, Palestinian Christian institutions, businesses, and loan owners may choose to provide services preferentially to Palestinians based on religious affiliation.[31] This focus on preservation over witness diminishes the church's prophetic role, reducing its mission to mere survival rather than confronting the challenges of the present. Yet, as reflected in Scripture and tradition, the church's mission has never depended on numerical strength. Such a focus contradicts the message of the Gospels and the legacy of the community of martyrs. Governments, armies, banks, and hedge funds measure their success in numbers and might; the church, however, is called to a different standard.

Patriarch Michel Sabbah articulated this in his first pastoral letter: "The greatness or the quality of the mission does not depend on the small or the large number of those who fulfil this mission. The mission is the same, irrespective of

---

31. See Loren D. Lybarger, "For Church or Nation? Islamism, Secular-Nationalism, and the Transformation of Christian Identities in Palestine," *Journal of the American Academy of Religion* 75, no. 4 (2007): 777–813; and Jack Munayer, "It's Time to Talk about Palestinian Evangelicals," *Mondoweiss*, 2022, https://mondoweiss.net/2022/04/its-time-to-talk-about-palestinian-evangelicals.

the numbers of those carrying it out."[32] He further empha-sized the weight of witness: "If there is plenty of salt, only a small quantity is needed to season the food. But if there is little of it, all is needed. Hence the earnestness of the task and mission to be fulfilled by a community of faithful which is not numerous, because the temptation to resign is great."[33] A Palestinian theology of martyrdom critiques the theol-ogy of survival prevalent in our community by shifting the focus from mere preservation to active agency. This agency is deeply rooted in faith, anchored in the conviction that true witness transcends both empire and death. It draws its strength from the power of the slain Lamb, whose liberation is not dependent on force or might but on transformative and redemptive love. It is through the suffering of martyr-dom — amid cruelty, injustice, and death — that we encounter the profound mystery of love, justice, and mercy, as ulti-mately revealed in the crucified Messiah.

While the theology of survival aims to preserve, it ulti-mately misguides, steering away from the authentic wit-ness to the living Christ that martyrs exemplify. As Khoury reminds us, "Christ did not establish the Church for its own sake, but for the sake of others."[34] Martyrdom and survival theology mirror the biblical story of Peter and Mary Mag-dalene. Peter, in his fear, denies Christ to save his life, while Mary Magdalene, unwavering in her faith, is steadfast in her witness to the crucifixion and the resurrection. Her testimony is one of courageous fidelity in the face of danger, embody-ing the true spirit of martyrdom. In times of genocide, this contrast between survival and martyrdom resonates with unparalleled poignancy. The stakes become unmistakably

---

32. Michel Sabbah, "First Pastoral Letters of Michel Sabbah," *Latin Patriarchate of Jerusalem*, 1988, https://www.lpj.org/storage/2023/12/14/1st-pastoral-letter-of-michel-sabbah-1591181230-docx.pdf.

33. Sabbah, "First Pastoral Letters."

34. Khoury, *Incarnation of Eastern Churches in the Arab Tent,* 39.

clear: to witness as Mary Magdalene did—to stand in the face of death.

Secondly, martyrdom, contextualized amid genocide and the global crackdown on the solidarity movement for Palestine, illuminates the element of community in discipleship. As previously noted, martyrdom carries legal connotations of bearing witness in a court of law. Since October 7, legal courts have supposedly served as platforms for witnessing truth and implementing justice. Institutions such as the International Court of Justice and the International Criminal Court have become arenas where testimony seeks to uncover truth and uphold accountability, or lie and gain impunity. The words of Christ to "follow me" and carry our own crosses entails choosing sides in the ongoing trial of Christ toward all and the trials against the oppressed with whom Christ identifies. Consequently, the choice is whether we choose to be false or true witnesses. It is important to note that this trial is ongoing, and thus, our witness ought to be credible through our testimonies, which are liberatory praxis. Therefore, as we are currently seeing mass mobilization and more voices struggling to achieve liberation, justice, and peace in Palestine and beyond, it is important to note which ones of them are credible, starting with ourselves.

While much can be said about martyrdom and discipleship in relating to the Palestinian context, we aim to focus here on the communal dimension of witness. The act of witnessing is inherently participatory, drawing us into a reality beyond ourselves and centered on Christ and the communion of witnesses. The martyrs of the past continue to speak into our present, as the martyred Bishop Oscar Romero once reflected, "If I am killed, I will resurrect in the people of El Salvador."[35] Indeed, martyrdom reminds us that our witness as a community is not about spokespeople or celebri-

---

35. Sobrino, *Witnesses to the Kingdom*, 186.

ties who represent the cause. Focusing on the celebrity icon would undermine the collective nature of our calling and the stepping stones for systematic change. Instead, our witness should be rooted in the movement of witnesses, grounded in shared purpose. For Palestinian Christians and other oppressed peoples, the communal aspect of witness carries particular urgency since our liberation and healing are interdependent. Given that our colonization is directly tied to Western powers, much of our effort has been directed at advocacy in the West—bearing witness to the plight of the oppressed and to the transformative message of the Gospel. While these efforts have yielded notable successes, there is a persistent temptation to prioritize external recognition over internal solidarity among oppressed peoples. This imbalance risks fragmenting and diluting our witness to one another.

Fragmentation manifests within our community of Palestinian Christian professional theologians, where we often work in isolation or within narrowly defined institutions and movements, even when our goals align. Like anywhere else in the world, certain loyalties, personalities, and conflicts have often been obstacles toward our communion—a communion that is not only seen in conferences, books, and webinars but one that resembles the early church in Acts, breaking bread together, devoting themselves to one another, and being of "one accord" (Acts 2:1). One must ask: how credible and valuable is our witness internationally if we fail to be witnesses to one another here in Palestine? Fragmentation manifests across multiple dimensions within the Palestinian Christian community, between those living in historic Palestine and the diaspora, within historic Palestine itself, and between Palestinian Christians and the broader Palestinian community, encompassing Muslims, seculars, and others. In this context, the theology of martyrdom calls us back to one another, reorienting us toward solidarity and collective healing. Here, we can look to St. Veronica and Simon of Cyrene as models, showing us how to help carry the cross and tend to the wounds of others, just as they did for Christ.

From a Palestinian perspective, martyrdom challenges us to contextualize communion in ways that reflect the realities of our struggle. This reimagined communion finds expression in the Arabic concept of Muthenna (Arabic for dual or pairing). Muthenna is a relational concept that can be understood as "without you, I am meaningless."[36] It describes a relational dynamic between two people, in which each maintains their individuality but exists in profound interdependence with the other. This relationship becomes integral to both, and each is transformed by it. This concept aligns closely with Ubuntu, the African philosophy of interdependence, which similarly affirms that our humanity is realized in relation to others. Munir Fasheh, drawing on the concept of Muthenna, applied it to create independent, nonhierarchical educational groups, fostering community-led epistemological learning and practice.[37] This approach, deeply rooted in relationality, offers a profound framework for Palestinian theology and can inspire broader transnational solidarity movements.

Within the context of martyrdom, the relational ethos of Muthenna extends beyond the living to encompass the martyrs of the past, whose witness continues to shape our identity and communal bonds. As a manifestation of the communal aspect of martyrdom, Muthenna invites us into a transformative communion where death does not have the final word. Through this lens, the martyrs' witness is not

36. Alice Gray, "The Roots of Resilience in Palestinian Culture," *The New Arab*, 2017, https://www.newarab.com/analysis/roots-resilience-palestinian-culture, quoting Munir Fasheh.

37. Munir Fasheh, "The Art of Neighbouring," *Mondoweiss*, 2016, https://medium.com/in-praise-of-scaling-down/the-art-of-neighboring-30fbd9dadfae.

merely a historical legacy but an enduring, dynamic force that shapes our present and future. As Sobrino aptly writes, "We must speak not only of a Church of martyrs, but of a Church built on its martyrs."[38]

Lastly, engaging with martyrdom in the Palestinian theological task offers a critical framework for discerning the "signs of the times" and the Kairos of our present moment, particularly in the context of the genocide. We need to go through similar processes that the pioneering generation of Palestinian theology went through during the First Intifada (1987), "the community must stop, think and meditate . . . [in order to] discover, understand, deepen its identity, vocation, mission, the meaning of its existence and the nature of its witness."[39] Contextuality, a method of doing theology that responds to the pressing realities of oppression and injustice, lies at the core of Palestinian theology. While Palestinian theology, most notably through Kairos Palestine and Palestinian liberation/contextual theology, has long served as a prophetic voice, the catastrophic reality in Gaza demands a renewal of this spirit. The martyrs and the immense suffering they represent must be seriously engaged to discern the will of God in this moment. This engagement is not a purely intellectual exercise but one that requires the full being of individuals and communities to confront the harsh realities. Theological knowledge cannot substitute for directly confronting this martial reality to discern God's presence in it.

The cries for help from Hind Rajab, "I am so scared, please come";[40] the poetry of Refaat Alareer, "If I must die

---

38. Sobrino, *Witnesses to the Kingdom,* 113.

39. Theology and the Local Church in the Holy Land, Al-Liqa Center for Religious and Heritage Studies in the Holy Land, 1987, 7.

40. Aljazeera, "The Take: The Story of Hind Rajab," AJEP Podcasts, 2024, https://www.aljazeera.com/podcasts/2024/2/19/the-take-the-story-of-hind-rajab, providing audio to Hind's call to emergency responders.

you must live";[41] and the overwhelming suffering in Gaza reflect the signs of our times. These voices, along with the persistent cries for liberation and justice, demand a direct and responsible engagement from theology. Gaza is not merely a backdrop for theological reflection. Gaza is the Kairos moment itself — a time when the martyrs bear witness to God's revelation and invite us to participate in it. The theological task is to take up these realities, discern their meaning, and embody them in praxis. Palestinian theology, with its liberative and contextual focus, has restored the relevance of faith in a world scarred by oppression. It has rediscovered the practical and political dimensions of the gospel, aiming "to make it meaningful to Palestinian Christians."[42] In this, the contribution of martyrdom is crucial, since "Liberation makes faith relevant, and martyrdom makes it credible."[43] Rational debates about God's sovereignty and goodness fail if detached from the costly praxis of liberation. Such abstract theodicies appear remote and untrustworthy to the oppressed, who instead place their trust in those willing to risk everything, even their own lives.

The theology of martyrdom does not seek to resolve the problem of truth through comprehensive explanations of God, nor does it aim to out-reason other religions or ideologies. Instead, it is grounded in a faith that persists without total understanding — a faith validated through the witness of martyrs. Their testimony compels theology to face reality directly, not as an escape into abstract concepts but as a transformative force to confront and change the world. Gaza's martyrs stand as signs of our time, urging Palestinian

41. Refaat Alaree, *If I Must Die: Poetry and Prose* (New York: OR Books, 2024).

42. Naim S. Ateek, *Justice and Only Justice: A Palestinian Theology of Liberation* (Maryknoll, NY: Orbis Books, 1989), 6.

43. Sobrino, *Witnesses to the Kingdom*, 125.

theology to continuously illuminate God's presence in the suffering and inspire redemptive vision and praxis.

Additional insights can further enrich Palestinian theology and its engagement with the realities on the ground, particularly through the lens of martyrdom. A Palestinian theology of martyrdom holds the potential to deeply resonate with Palestinian Muslims by drawing on shared cultural, historical, and spiritual understandings of sacrifice, justice, and resistance.[44] In Islam, the concept of martyrdom, or shahada, carries profound significance, symbolizing a witness to faith, truth, and the pursuit of justice. For both Palestinian Muslims and Christians, the shared experiences of oppression, displacement, and resistance under occupation provide a strong foundation for solidarity and unity. In this context, martyrdom transcends theological boundaries, becoming a collective expression of resistance and a witness to injustice. Both traditions may view martyrdom as embodying courage, selflessness, and a profound connection to the divine, creating a powerful point of interfaith resonance. This resonance can extend beyond Muslim and Christian communities in Palestine, offering a theology that speaks to others who share the collective struggle for justice. By contextualizing martyrdom to engage those outside the Christian tradition and incorporating diverse perspectives, this theology has the potential to serve as a unifying and inclusive articulation of resistance and hope for all Palestinians and people living between the river and the sea.

In this brief reflection, we have sought to contextualize martyrdom within Scripture and tradition, bringing it into dialogue with the Palestinian reality. Specifically, in addressing martyrdom amid the genocide in Gaza, we propose three

---

44. "Creative resistance," as identified by Mitri Raheb. Mitri Raheb, *Faith in the Face of Empire: The Bible through Palestinian Eyes* (Maryknoll, NY: Orbis Books, 2014).

key insights for Palestinian theology: first, to challenge and move beyond a theology of survival; second, to emphasize the communal dimension of witness as integral to its practice; and third, to incorporate the martial reality and the suffering of the oppressed into the very method and orientation of theology. This integration is essential for discerning the signs of our time and embracing the Kairos moment with authenticity and urgency.

Conclusion

The stakes in articulating Palestinian theology are undeniable. We must acknowledge our own privilege and its limitations in understanding and expressing a theology of martyrdom. Writing this chapter from Jerusalem, we are not under the same imminent threat of death faced by our brothers and sisters in Gaza or parts of the West Bank. The theology of martyrdom is a multifaceted reality for Palestinians, yet our shared experience and the unfolding events in Palestine demand that we engage with it as an essential and communal theological task.

Theologians worldwide must confront the questions: How does one do theology in the shadow of genocide? How do we understand discipleship to Christ in such times? How do we bear witness? These are not abstract questions but urgent calls to action, for no theology claiming to be for and from the oppressed can afford to ignore Gaza. Lip service is not enough. The task is to engage with the magnitude of suffering honestly, directly, and with unwavering commitment. We ought to wrestle theologically as the Palestinian theologian Geries Khoury did during the First Intifada, when, as today, "the souls of the martyrs fill the skies of Palestine with the fragrance of heroism and sacrifice."[45]

---

45. Geries Khoury, *The Intifada of Heaven and the Intifada of Earth* (Nazareth: Al-Hakim, 1989), 8.

A Palestinian theology of martyrdom challenges the theology of survival that prioritizes preservation over witness, echoing Rafiq Khoury's prayer: "Lord, if we want to be witnesses to the resurrection, let us not be guardians of relics and graves."[46] Moreover, the theology of martyrdom calls us to a communal form of witness necessary for healing, liberation, and reconciliation. Lastly, the theology of martyrdom demands that we discern the signs of our times through the martyrs and the suffering of the innocent in Palestine. Much remains to be reflected upon, but the theology of martyrdom offers a spiritual and political framework for confronting the immense challenges that we face.

Even as the future appears grim, we hold fast to the hope that our witness will endure, resisting the allure of comfort and defying the empire's oppressive logic by embracing our own crosses. The true power of martyrdom lies not only in its testament to suffering but in its courageous declaration that life, truth, and liberation triumph even in the shadow of death.

---

46. Khoury, *Incarnation of Eastern Churches in the Arab Tent*, 39. Translation from Arabic by the authors.

Contributors

Yousef Kamal AlKhouri, PhD, is a Palestinian Christian theologian born in Gaza, where his family has a centuries-long heritage serving in the Orthodox Church. He is an assistant professor of biblical studies at Bethlehem Bible College and its academic dean. AlKhouri serves on the board of Kairos Palestine, the steering committee of Christ at the Checkpoint, and is a founding member of the Academic Alliance for Interfaith Dialogue in Palestine.

Azmera Hammouri-Davis is a writer, poet, and theologian from Kea'au, Hawai'i. The granddaughter of a Nakba survivor from Hebron, Palestine, she authored *Breaking the Boxes: Poems for Keeping Hope Alive When Your Faith Is Fractured.* Azmera's work also appears in *Sojourners, Interfaith America, Mondoweiss,* and the *Journal of Interreligious Studies.* She is a Fulbright Performing Artist, MICAH Ministry Fellow, Harvard Divinity School graduate, and creator of The Capoethic Method.

Lamma Mansour, DPhil, is a Christian Palestinian from Nazareth. She has a doctorate and a master's degree in social policy and intervention from the University of Oxford, and a BSc in psychology from the University of Haifa. Her research focuses on young people in Israel-Palestine, and has been published in leading journals in the field. Alongside her academic work, Lamma serves in her local church in Nazareth and has written and spoken on the intersection of faith and society in local and global outlets.

Daniel S. Munayer is based in Jerusalem and is the executive director of Musalaha, an organization promoting reconciliation between Palestinians and Israelis. Prior, he co-founded Lighthouse Relief in Greece, addressing the refugee crisis on Lesvos Island, and has worked with the Danish Refugee Council and Nonviolent Peaceforce in humanitarian responses in Greece and Iraq. Daniel holds an MBA from Durham University and a BA in international relations and religious studies from American University in Washington, DC.

John S. Munayer is a Palestinian theologian from and based in Jerusalem, and a PhD student at the University of Edinburgh. He works in the field of interreligious peacebuilding and justice in Jerusalem, and helped found the *Journal of Palestinian Christianity* at Bethlehem Bible College. John holds degrees from King's College London, the University of Edinburgh, and VU University Amsterdam.

Samuel S. Munayer, a Palestinian theologian from and based in Jerusalem, holds a BA in theology and philosophy from Durham University and an MA in Middle Eastern politics from the University of Exeter, where he was supervised by Ilan Pappé. He currently works as a humanitarian professional in the occupied Palestinian territories. Samuel has authored several articles, including "Decolonizing Palestinian Liberation Theology: New Methods, Sources, and Voices." He is the co-author of the forthcoming book *The Palestinian Christ*.

Shadia Qubti has worked in peacebuilding parachurch organizations in Israel and Palestine for fifteen years. As a

Palestinian Christian theologian currently serving as community engagement animator at Trinity Grace United Church in Vancouver, she weaves together lived experience, contextual theology, and decolonial practice. Her work focuses on cultivating spaces where marginalized voices, particularly those of women, can emerge and flourish, as demonstrated through her co-founding of the *Women Behind the Wall* podcast.

Marah Sarji is a PhD student in theology, ethics, and politics at Princeton Theological Seminary. Born and raised in Nazareth, Marah grew up among the diverse Christian traditions and was involved in leading Palestinian justice-oriented initiatives. Marah's research focuses on Palestinian women's role in preserving and interpreting Palestinian theology, specifically through the tradition of St. Barbara, in the wider context of Palestinian contextual theology and Arabic Christianity in the region.

Index

147